Workbook for
IELTS

Workbook for IELTS

발행일	2018년 7월 18일

지은이	전 현 선		
펴낸이	손 형 국		
펴낸곳	(주)북랩		
편집인	선일영	편집	권혁신, 오경진, 최승헌, 최예은, 김경무
디자인	이현수, 김민하, 한수희, 김윤주, 허지혜	제작	박기성, 황동현, 구성우, 정성배
마케팅	김회란, 박진관, 조하라		
출판등록	2004. 12. 1(제2012-000051호)		
주소	서울시 금천구 가산디지털 1로 168, 우림라이온스밸리 B동 B113, 114호		
홈페이지	www.book.co.kr		
전화번호	(02)2026-5777	팩스	(02)2026-5747

ISBN	979-11-6299-208-1 13740(종이책)	979-11-6299-209-8 15740(전자책)

이 도서의 국립중앙도서관 출판예정도서목록(CIP)은 서지정보유통지원시스템 홈페이지(http://seoji.nl.go.kr)와 국가자료공동목록시스템(http://www.nl.go.kr/kolisnet)에서 이용하실 수 있습니다.
(CIP제어번호: CIP2018021231)

(주)북랩 성공출판의 파트너

북랩 홈페이지와 패밀리 사이트에서 다양한 출판 솔루션을 만나 보세요!

홈페이지 book.co.kr   •   **블로그** blog.naver.com/essaybook   •   **원고모집** book@book.co.kr

IELTS 수험생이라면 반드시 마스터해야 할 영작의 기술

Workbook for
IELTS

전현선 지음
London IELTS Academy

시험에 자주 출제되는 24개 주제
단어부터 문장, 문단 구성 제공
에세이 라이팅 가이드

북랩 book Lab

머리말/아이엘츠(IELTS)를 준비하시는 분들께

무엇보다도 라이팅(Writing)에 대한 접근이 어렵다는 것을 발견하실 겁니다. 처음부터 에세이(Essay) 250자를 작성하는 것은 쉽지 않습니다. 단어나 구문과 더불어 문장 구성력이 없으면 제대로 된 에세이를 작성할 수가 없습니다. 그런 문제점에 대한 대비로 에세이 작성에 필요한 단어 또는 구문을 주제별로 정리해 봤습니다. 제 교재 『IELTS Easy Writing』에 이미 나와 있는 단어나 구문들도 있지만 같은 주제 다른 아이디어로 에세이를 작성하고자 하는 분들을 위해서 좀 더 폭넓은 자료를 제공했습니다. 전반적으로 이 책을 공부하시면 IELTS에서 중요시하는 패러프레이즈(Paraphrase)에 대한 문제 또한 해결하실 수 있고 라이팅뿐만 아니라 리딩/리스닝/스피킹(Reading/Listening/Speaking)에도 많은 도움이 될 것이라 확신합니다

학습순서

1. 단어나 구문 Practice
2. 문장 Practice
3. 같은 주제로 Essay 작성
4. 제시된 기출 문제로 Essay 작성
5. ieltseasywriting.com에 첨삭 요청

저자 전현선(London IELTS Academy/Writing class 운영 중)

Academy

Task 1: Graph(at least 150)

Task 2: Essay(at least 250)

General

Task 1: Letter(at least 150)

Task 2: Essay(at least 250)

채점기준

Ⅰ. Task Response(요구사항 부합) (25%)

Ⅱ. Coherence and Cohesion(논리 정연함과 언어의 결속성) (25%)

Ⅲ. Lexical Resource(어휘력) (25%)

Ⅳ. Grammatical Range and Accuracy(문법의 다양성과 정확성) (25%)

TIP (IELTS 공식안내)

1. Writing 시험은 정답을 요하는 시험이 아니라 영어로 주어진 정보를 전달하고 의견을 표현하는 능력을 평가합니다.
2. Task 1은 150 단어, Task 2는 250 단어 이상을 작성하셔야 하며, 이보다 짧게 작성할 경우에는 감점됩니다.
3. Writing 답안지 작성 시 문제의 문장을 그대로 적는다면 그 부분은 단어 수에서 제외됩니다. 응시자 본인의 표현으로 작성해야 합니다.
4. Academic Task 1에서는 주어진 데이터를 임의로 해석하거나 자료 결과를 추측하지 말고 주어진 자료만을 가지고 기술해야 합니다.
5. Academic Task 2에서는 작성자의 논점과 견해를 뒷받침할 수 있는 내용이나 주장을 예를 들면서 작성하고 결론에는 앞 문단에서 작성한 내용을 바탕으로 맺음합니다.
6. Task 1 작성에는 20분을, Task 2 작성에는 40분을 권유합니다. 각 Task에서 처음 5분 동안은 작성할 글을 구성하고, 마지막 5분 동안에는 작성한 글을 읽으며 실수한 부분은 없는지 확인합니다.

/www.ieltskorea.org 제공

Contents

Unit 1

Technology

Advanced technology has been beneficial to human life. However, there are also disadvantages of modern technology. Describe the merits and demerits.

ESSENTIAL VOCA

INTRODUCTION

최근에	in recent years/in recent times/recently
현대 기술/첨단 기술	advanced(developed/progressed/cutting edge/state-of-the-art/high-end) technology
기술 혁신	technological innovation
엄청난 변화	a sea of changes/a big change
눈부신 발전을 이루다	achieve(accomplish) a breakthrough
대부분은/주로	predominantly/mainly/mostly
중요한	imperative/essential/vital/important/fundamental/significant
일반적인 믿음과 달리	contrary to(as opposed to) common belief
~인지 아닌지에 대한 의문을 제기하다	raise the question of(cast doubt on) whether S+V
이 쟁점이 대중의 높은 관심을 받아 오고 있다	this issue has been a high profile
부정적으로	negatively/adversely/in the negative
장단점들	pros and cons/advantages and disadvantages/merits and demerits/strengths and weaknesses
자세히 설명하다	spell out/elaborate on/explain in full detail
다음과 같이	as follows

BODY 1(positive factors)

한편으로는	on the one hand/meanwhile
삶을 편리하고 편안하게 하다	make people's lives more convenient and comfortable
기술적인 측면에서	in terms of(with respect to/when it comes to) technology
기술 발전 덕택으로	with the help of(thanks to) technological development
긍정적인 면에서는	on the bright(positive/affirmative) side
많은/다수의 사람	plenty of(a number of/a slew of/loads of) people
~에 대단히 기여하다	make a considerable contribution to(contribute a great deal to)+Ⓝ
광범위하게 미치는 영향	a far-reaching(far-flung) effect(influence/implication)
언제 어디서든지	anytime, anyplace/anyplace and anytime
시간과 장소에 상관없이	regardless of(without reference to) time and place
장벽들 없이	without barriers(obstacles)
~와 연락하다	get in touch with/make a contact with/contact with~
노사	labor and management/labor and business
작업장에서 복잡하고 위험한 공정에서	in complicated and dangerous process at a workplace
과거에는 손으로 그들의 일을 하다	do their work manually in the past
최소한의 노력과 시간으로	with minimum effort and time
상당한 시간을 절약하다	save a considerable(great) amount of time
가전제품	home appliances/household equipment
가전제품 도움 없이	without the aid of home appliances
집안일을 하다	do housework/do house chores/do household chores
지루하고 피곤한 일	tiring and tiresome work
인공 지능	AI(artificial intelligence)
컴퓨터화	computerization
광범위한 컴퓨터 사용	the extensive use of computer
통신 기술을 가능하게 하다	facilitate(enable) communication technology
환경친화적이고 깨끗한 에너지나 서비스를 공급하는 기술	green technology
A에게 B를 제공하다	provide(supply/furnish) A with B/provide(supply/furnish) B to(for) A

가령 ~라면	provided that(providing that) S+V
생산성을 높이다	raise(increase/promote) productivity
수많은 상황들	countless(numberless) situations(circumstances/conditions)
경쟁사회에서	in a competitive society
더욱이	furthermore/moreover/what is more
예를 들어	to give an example/for instance/for example/to illustrate/for one thing/to cite one example
A뿐만 아니라 B도	B as well as A/not only A but also B
잘 알려진 사실이다	it is a well-known fact that S+V
~에 상당한 영향을 끼치다	have an immense(significant/considerable) impact(influence/effect) on~
~에 긍정적인 영향을 끼치다	have a positive(affirmative/beneficial) effect(influence/impact) on~
~에 유익하다/도움이 되다	be of benefit to(be of help to)+Ⓝ
기술을 이용하다	make use of(take advantage of/harness/employ) technology

BODY 2(negative factors)

그와는 반대로	on the contrary/on the other hand/in contrast/by contrast/on the flip side
기술적 발전과 관련해서	associated with(related to/linked to) technological development
~와 비교하여	compared to/in comparison with/as compared with~
~하는 경향이 있다	have a tendency to/tend to/be inclined to/be prone to/be liable to~
컴퓨터에 대한 의존	dependence(reliance) on a computer
컴퓨터가 고장 나다	a computer is broken/a computer breaks down
기술적 결함에 직면하다	face(confront/encounter) technical imperfection(deficiency/flaw/defection)
누군가를 혼란에 빠트리다	throw somebody into confusion(chaos/mess)
중대한 후유증	a grave aftereffect(aftermath)
~에 중대한 위협을 가하다	pose grave threats to(threaten/pose serious risks to)+Ⓝ
~에 큰 타격을 주다/큰 피해를 주다	take a toll on~/wreck havoc on~
실업을 부추기다	accelerate(fuel/encourage/instigate) unemployment(joblessness)
발달된 기계와 정밀한 설비들	advanced machines and elaborate(delicate) equipment

노동력을 대체하다	replace labor (work)force
사회적 문제들을 야기하나(초래하나)	lead to(give rise to/result in/bring about) social problems
과실, 범죄 그리고 심지어 자살과 같은	such as delinquencies, crimes and even suicides
이러한 경우에서 보여진 것처럼/이처럼	as seen in this case/like this/with this
따라서/그러므로	consequently/as a result/thus/therefore/hence/in this context
~에 대해 걱정하다	be concerned about/be worried about~
~에 해로운 영향을 주다	have a harmful(detrimental/adverse/pernicious) influence(impact/effect) on~

CONCLUSION

요약하자면	to sum up/in conclusion/to conclude/in short
위에서 언급한 것처럼	as stated above/as mentioned above
부정적인 영향	negative impacts(effects/influences)
훨씬 더 ~할 것 같다	be far(much) more likely to~
적절하게	appropriately/properly/adequately/correctly
전적으로	entirely/completely/fully/totally
~을 잘(더 잘/최대한) 이용하다	make good(better/the best) use of~

SENTENCE PRACTICE

INTRODUCTION

1. 최근에 현대기술은 엄청난 변화를 가져오고 있고 그것은 대부분의 사람들의 삶에 긍정적이다.

_____

_____

2. 그러나, 일반적인 믿음과 달리, 어떤 사람들은 기술은 인간에게 부정적인 영향을 준다고 여전히 주장한다.

_____

_____

3. 이 에세이는 현대기술의 장점들과 단점들을 고려할 것이다.

_____

_____

BODY 1

1. 한편으로는, 현대기술이 사람들의 삶을 더욱더 편리하고 편안하게 한다.

_____

_____

2. 산업 로봇들과 같은 발전된 기술 혁신 덕택으로, 노동자들은 작업장에서 복잡하고 위험한 공정에서 손으로 일을 할 필요가 없다.

_____

_____

3. 이것은 노사를 안전하고 생산적이게 만든다.

_____

_____

4. 집안일의 경우에, 과거에 주부들은 집안일을 가전기기의 도움 없이 했고, 그것은 지루하고 피곤한 것이었다.

_____

_____

5. 다행히, 세탁기와 로봇청소기 같은 다양한 종류의 가전제품의 발전은 그들이 최소한의 노력으로 집안일을 할 수 있게 한다.

_____

_____

6. 그것은 그들이 더 생산적인 일을 하고 현대사회에서 그들의 삶을 즐길 수 있도록 하고 있다.

_____

_____

7. 이처럼, 사람들은 현대기술의 영향을 긍정적으로 받고 있다.

_____

_____

BODY 2

1. 이에 반해서, 기술적 발전과 관련해서 소홀히 할 수 없는 단점들이 있다.

_____

_____

2. 첫째로, 사람들은 기술에 너무 의지하는 경향이 있다.

_____

_____

3. 그리고, 이것은 기술적인 결함에 직면했을 때 사람들을 혼란에 빠트릴 수 있다.

_____

_____

4. 예를 들면, 만약 컴퓨터가 고장 난다면, 대부분의 사람은 더 이상 많은 일들을 할 수 없다.

_____

_____

5. 이러한 기계에 대한 의존은 너무 강해서 사람들은 그것의 도움 없이는 일을 수행할 수 없다.

_____

_____

6. 이러한 경우에서 보여진 것처럼, 사람들의 삶은 현대기술에 과도하게 지배될 수 있다.

_____

_____

7. 둘째로, 기술적 발전은 실업을 가속화시킨다.

_____

_____

8. 그것은 발달된 기계와 정밀한 설비들이 많은 직장에서 노동력을 대체하고 있기 때문이다.

_____

_____

9. 그리고 이것은 과실, 범죄 그리고 심지어 자살과 같은 사회적 문제를 초래하고 있다.

_____

_____

10. 그러므로, 발전된 기술은 현대사회에 악영향을 줄 수 있다.

_____

_____

CONCLUSION

1. 결론적으로, 현대기술이 부정적인 효과를 가지고 있지만, 그것은 더 긍정적인 측면들을 가지고 있는 것 같다.

_____

_____

2. 그러므로, 만약 사람들이 발전된 기술을 현명하고 적절하게 잘 이용한다면, 그것은 사람들의 삶과 사회에 전적으로 유용할 수 있다.

_____

_____

ANSWER

INTRODUCTION

1. In recent years, developed technology has brought a sea of changes, which is predominantly positive, to people's lives.

2. Some people, having said that, still argue that, contrary to common belief, technology affects humans negatively.

3. This essay will consider the merits and demerits of contemporary technology.

BODY 1

1. On the one hand, modern technology makes people's lives much more convenient and comfortable.

2. With the help of advanced technological innovation like industrial robots, laborers do not need to do their work manually in complicated and dangerous process at workplaces.

3. It makes labor and management secure and productive.

4. In the case of housework, homemakers in the past did housework without the aid of home appliances, which was tiring and tiresome.

5. Luckily, the development of various kinds of household equipment like washing machines and robot vacuum cleaners enables them to do household chores with minimal effort.

6. It allows them to do more productive work and enjoys their lives in modern society.

7. Like this, people are influenced positively by current technology.

BODY 2

1. On the other hand, there are drawbacks associated with technological development that should not be ignored.

2. Firstly, people have a tendency to depend on technology too much

3. , and this could throw them into confusion when faced technical imperfection.

4. For example, when computers break down, most people are no longer able to do many things.

5. Their dependence on the machine is so high that they cannot perform tasks without its assistance.

6. As seen in this case, people's lives can be substantially controlled by modern technology.

7. Secondly, technological progress accelerates unemployment.

8. It is because advanced machines and precision equipment have replaced the labor force in many workplaces

9. , and this has led to social problems such as delinquencies, crimes, and even suicides.

10. Therefore, the developed technology could have adverse effects on modern society.

CONCLUSION

1. In conclusion, modern technology has negative impacts, but it is more likely to have positive points.

2. In this context, if people make good use of advanced technology wisely and appropriately, it can be entirely useful to people's lives and societies.

PREVIOUS TEST

> **1.** It is inevitable that traditional cultures will be lost as technology develops. Technology and traditional culture are incompatible. To what extent do you agree or disagree with this statement?
>
> **2.** In the last 20 years, there have been significant developments in the field of information technology. However, these development in IT are likely to have more negative effects in the future.
> To what extent do you agree with this view?
>
> **3.** Information technology is changing many aspects of our lives and now dominates our home, leisure and work activities. To what extent do the benefits of information technology outweigh the disadvantages?

** 첨삭은 ieltseasywriting.com

2. Mobile phone

It is true that the use of mobile phone has been on the rise, and it also has great influences on people's lives. What is your opinion of using a mobile phone?

ESSENTIAL VOCA

INTRODUCTION

최근에	in recent years/in recent times/recently
기술의 획기적인 발전	a breakthrough in technology
현대 기술/첨단 기술	advanced(developed/cutting-edge/state-of-the-art) technology
모바일 폰의 발명과 함께	with the invention of mobile phones
모바일 폰 덕택으로	with the help of(thanks to) a mobile phone
편리하고 편안한	convenient and comfortable
그러나	having said that/however/yet/but/though
~인지 아닌지에 대한 의문을 제기하다	raise the question of(pose the question of/cast doubt on) whether S+V
이점들	benefits/good points/virtues/merits/advantages
단점들	demerits/disadvantages/drawbacks/bad points/downsides
아래와 같이	as follows
분석하다	analyze/make an analysis
자세히 설명하다	spell out/elaborate on/explain in full detail
다음은 이유들이다	the following are the reasons

BODY 1(positive aspects)

우선	first of all/to begin with/above all
~에 대해 말하자면	in the case of/in terms of/when it comes to/in light of/with respect to
모바일 폰 덕택으로	with the help of(thanks to) a mobile phone
긍정적인 면에서는	on the positive(affirmative/bright) side
필수품	a must/a necessity/a must-have
거리의 제한 없이	without distance barriers(obstacles)
빠르고 확실하게	quickly and reliably
대인의사소통	interpersonal communication
~와 대화하다	communicate(have a word/talk) with~
~와 연락하다	contact/get in touch with/make contact with~
위급한 경우에	in case of emergency situations
어려움을 해결하다	cope with(deal with/handle) difficulties(hardships/troubles)
애플리케이션으로 언어와 요리법을 배우다	learn languages and recipes with applications
인터넷상에서	on the Internet/online
모바일 결제	mobile payments
재정과 기술의 합성어	Fintech(financial+technology)
입출금 거래를 가능하게 하다	facilitate(enable) deposit and withdraw transactions
은행을 대신하여	on behalf of(in place of/in lieu of) the bank
은행 업무를 수행하다	conduct(carry out/perform) banking services
이동하는 시간과 비용을 절약하다	save time and cost for commuting
시간과 장소에 상관없이	regardless of(without reference to) time and place
최소한의 노력과 시간으로	with minimum effort and time
인터넷을 검색하다	surf(search) the Internet(web)
통신 기술	communication technology
소셜 미디어	social media
소셜 네트워크 서비스	SNS(social network service)
가상공간	virtual space

사회적 상호작용	social interaction
다양한 정보	a broad(wide/great) range(variety) of information
최신정보	up-to-date information
많은/다수의	plenty of/a number of/a lot of
유익한	constructive/beneficial/valuable/advantageous
사람의 삶의 방식에 유익하다	be of benefit to(be of help to) people's way of lives
~에 긍정적인 영향을 끼치다	have(exert) positive(affirmative/beneficial) effects(influences/impacts) on~
~에 상당한 영향을 끼치다	have(exert) immense(significant/considerable) impacts(influences/effects) on
눈부신 발전을 이루다	achieve(accomplish) a breakthrough

BODY 2(negative aspects)

그와는 반대로	on the contrary/on the other hand/on the flip side
사실상	in fact/as a matter of fact/actually/in reality/virtually
~에 해로운 영향을 주다	have(exert) harmful(detrimental/adverse/pernicious) influences(impacts/effects) on~
쓸모 없는 정보	useless(worthless/unhelpful/valueless) information
무분별한 정보	indiscriminate(thoughtless/indiscreet) information
~로 넘쳐나다	teem with/rich in/be full of/be flooded of
~에 접근하다	have access to(get access to/access/approach)+Ⓝ
저속하고 선정적인 자료들	obscene and sexual(suggestive) materials
넘쳐나는 사진들과 영상들	a flood of pictures and videos/overflowing pictures and videos
다양한 정보를 퍼트리다	disseminate a wide(whole) variety(range) of information
노출되다	be exposed to(be revealed to/be disclosed to/get exposure to)+Ⓝ
사생활을 침해하다	infringe on(invade/intrude/violate) one's privacy
인증번호/비밀번호	PIN number
사이버 공격과 범죄	cyber-attacks and cyber-crimes
많은 범죄들	a large number of(great numbers/plenty of/many) crimes
범죄자들	criminals/offenders/culprits

휴대폰과 관련된 범죄들	crimes related to(associated with/involved with) mobile phones
은행계좌를 해킹하다	hack a bank account
개인의 정보를 캐내려는 사기성 행위	phishing
계속되는 위험	an ongoing(lasting) danger
~에 중대한 위협을 가하다	pose grave(serious) threats(risks) to+Ⓝ
A를 위협하다	danger A/threaten A/put A in danger/imperil A
정보를 유출하다	leak(disclose/divulge/drain) information
개인정보를 모으다	collect(accumulate/gather) personal information
중독성이 있는	addictive
인터넷에 중독되다	get addicted to(be poisoned with/addict oneself to/be addicted to) the Internet
연구들은 또한 확신하고(보여주고) 있다	studies have also confirmed(showed) that S+V
보고되고 있다	it is reported that S+V
학습을 방해하다	disturb(interrupt/interfere) learning
사실을 왜곡하다	distort(strain) the truth(the fact)
인간의 권리를 침해하다	violate(infringe on/invade) human rights
휴대폰의 사용에 관해서	regarding(as regards/concerning/as to) the use of a mobile phone
과도한 온라인 사회화	excessive online socialization
휴대폰에 대한 의존성	dependence(reliance) on mobile phones
휴대폰에 익숙하다	get(be) accustomed(used) to mobile phones
휴대폰에 의지하다	rely on(depend on/be dependent on/resort to) mobile phones
휴대폰 이용자들에게 큰 타격을 주다/큰 피해를 주다	wreck havoc on(take a toll on) mobile phone users

CONCLUSION

요약하자면	to sum up/in conclusion/to conclude/in short
A를 고려하다	take A into account(consideration)/consider A
사람의 안전을 위협하다	endanger(threaten) people's security
A에게 B를 제공하다	provide(supply/furnish) A with B/provide(supply/furnish) B to(for) A

생산성을 높이다	increase(raise/promote) productivity
중요한	imperative/essential/vital/significant/fundamental
적절하고 현명하게	appropriately and sensibly/reasonably and wisely
이점들이 단점들보다 훨씬 크다	the advantages far outweigh the disadvantages
결론은 ~이다	the bottom line is that S+V

SENTENCE PRACTICE

INTRODUCTION

1. 다양한 현대 기술 발전이 있어 왔다.

_____

_____

2 그리고, 이 도움으로 오늘날 대부분의 사람들은 그들의 삶을 더 편리하고 편안하게 하기 위해서 휴대폰을 사용해 오고 있다.

_____

_____

3. 그러나, 일부 사람들은 휴대폰이 유용한지 아닌지에 대한 의문을 제기한다.

_____

_____

4. 다음 토론은 휴대폰 사용의 장단점에 관한 것이다.

_____

_____

BODY 1

1. 휴대폰의 가장 큰 이점은 사람들이 그것을 가지고 다니는 한 거리의 제한 없이 효율적으로 대화하는 것이다.

_____

_____

2. 대부분의 사람들에게, 휴대폰은 필수품이 되고 있다.

_____

_____

3. 그들은 시간과 장소에 관계없이 그들의 가족들이나 친구들과 연락하기를 원하기 때문이다.

_____

_____

4. 더욱이, 긴급한 상황에서 그들은 휴대폰으로 911에 전화함으로써 어려움에 대처할 수 있다.

_____

_____

5. 다른 이점은 사람들은 스마트폰 애플리케이션을 가지고 많은 것들을 해결할 수 있다는 것이다.

_____

_____

6. 다운로드한 애플리케이션들로 그들은 새로운 언어 그리고 요리법들을 배울 수 있다.

_____

_____

7. 또한 온라인 쇼핑 사이트는 모바일 플랫폼을 가지고 있어서 그것은 소비자들에게 그들이 온라인에서 쇼핑할 때 모바일 결제를 가능하게 한다.

_____

_____

8. 요즘, 핀 테크(재정+기술)는 고객들이 은행을 대신해 휴대폰을 가지고 입출금 거래와 같은 은행 업무를 수행하게 한다.

_____

_____

9. 이것은 그들이 오고 가는 시간과 비용을 절약할 수 있게 한다.

_____

_____

10. 이와 같이, 휴대폰의 사용은 사람들의 삶의 방식에 매우 유익하다.

_____

_____

BODY 2

1. 그와는 반대로, 휴대폰의 사용은 사용자의 삶에 해로운 영향을 줄 수 있다.

_____

_____

2. 첫째, 휴대폰은 다양한 정보를 가지고 있지만 또한 쓸모 없고 무분별한 정보들로 가득 차 있다.

_____

_____

3. 특히, 어린이들이나 청소년들은 외설적이고 선정적인 자료들에 접근할 수 있다. 이러한 것들은 그들의 사회 정서적 발달에 전혀 도움이 뇌시 않는다.

_____

_____

4. 더욱이, 스마트폰에서의 모바일 애플리케이션은 범죄에 사용될 수 있다.

_____

_____

5. 범죄자들은 사진, 집주소 그리고 심지어 은행계좌들 같은 개인정보들을 얻기 위해 몇 가지 애플리케이션을 해킹하는 것으로 알려져 있다.

_____

_____

6. 사실상, 휴대폰과 관련된 많은 사건들이 있다.

_____

_____

7. 예를 들면, 요즘 SMS(짧은 메시지 서비스) 피싱이 종종 발생하고 있다.

_____

_____

8. 그것은 사람들을 유인하고 그들의 정보를 모으기 위해 문자 메시지를 이용한다.

_____

_____

9. 그러므로, 이러한 부정적인 면들이 간과되어서는 안 된다.

_____

_____

CONCLUSION

1. 결론은 이 모든 것을 고려해 볼 때, 휴대폰의 효율적인 사용은 우리에게 편리함을 제공하고 일상생활에서 생산성을 증가시킨다.

_____

_____

2. 그러나, 만약 현명하게 사용하지 않으면, 그들은 또한 사생활을 침해하고 사람들의 안전을 위협할 수 있다.

_____

_____

3. 따라서, 휴대폰을 적절하고 현명하게 사용하는 것이 중요하다.

_____

_____

ANSWER

INTRODUCTION

1. There have been numerous modern technological advances,

2. and with this help, most people today have used a mobile phone to make their lives more convenient and comfortable.

3. Some, having said that, raise a question of whether the mobile phone is beneficial or not.

4. The following discussion is the pros and cons of the usage of cell phones.

BODY 1

1. The biggest benefit of mobile phones is for people to communicate efficiently without distance barriers so long as individuals carry them.

2. For most people, mobile phones have become a must.

3. It is because they want to contact their families or friends by phone regardless of time and place.

4. Moreover, in the case of emergency situations, they can cope with difficulties by dialing 911 with a mobile phone.

5. Another merit is that people can solve many things with smartphone applications.

6. By download applications, they can learn new languages and recipes.

7. Also, online shopping sites have mobile platforms which make it possible for customers to use mobile payments when they shop online.

8. Nowadays, Fintech(financial+technology) allows customers to conduct banking services like deposit and withdraw transactions on behalf of the bank with mobiles phones.

9. It enables them to save time and cost for commuting.

10. Like this, using mobile phones is of great benefit to people's way of life.

BODY 2

1. On the contrary, the use of mobile phones can have a pernicious effect on people's lives.

2. First, mobile phones have a broad range of information, but they are flooded with useless and indiscriminate data as well.

3. In particular, children and the youth could get access to a lot of obscene and sexual materials indiscreetly with their mobile phones, which is of no help to their social and emotional development.

4. Furthermore, mobile applications on smartphones can be used for crimes.

5. It is reported that criminals hack some applications to acquire personal information like photos, home address, and even bank account.

6. In fact, there are a large number of crimes related to mobile phones.

7. For instance, nowadays, SMS(short message service) phishing happens at times.

8. It uses text messages to induce people and to collect their information.

9. Therefore, these downsides should not be overlooked.

CONCLUSION

1. In conclusion, taking all these into consideration, the efficient use of mobile phones provides us with convenience, increasing productivity in everyday lives.

2. However, if now wisely used, they can also violate our privacy and endanger people's security.

3. Thus, it is imperative to use mobile phones appropriately and sensibly.

PREVIOUS TEST

1. Some people think that mobile phones should be banned in public places like libraries, shops and on public transport.
   To what extent do you agree or disagree with this statement?

2. The dangers and complexities of the modern world have made the mobile phone an absolute necessity for children.
   To what extent do you agree or disagree?

3. There are social, medical, and technical problems associated with the use of mobile phones.
   Do you agree the problems of mobile phones outweigh the benefits?

** 첨삭은 ieltseasywriting.com

3. Computer

Computers have been made use of the way people study. Do the advantages of using computers as a study tool outweigh the disadvantages?

ESSENTIAL VOCA

INTRODUCTION

컴퓨터의 출현	the advent of computer
기술 혁신	technological innovation
컴퓨터의 광범위한 사용	the broad(extensive/widespread/wide) use of computer
상당한 변화	a sea of changes/significant(considerable/comparative) changes
최첨단 제품들	cutting-edge(state-of-the-art/high-end) products
필수품	a must-have/a necessity/essential goods
다양한 지식	a broad(wide/great) range(variety) of knowledge
지식을 얻다	acquire(gain/obtain/get) knowledge
부정적인 측면들	negative factors(aspects)
요인들/원인들	factors/aspects/causes/influences
단점들	disadvantages/demerits/bad points/drawbacks/weaknesses
장점들	advantages/merits/good points/benefits/strengths
자세히 설명하다	spell out/elaborate on/explain in full detail
다음과 같이	as follows

BODY 1(positive factors)

우선	first of all/to begin with/first and foremost
컴퓨터와 관련하여	concerning(regarding/as regards/with regard to/as respects) computers
많은 시간과 노력을 절약하다	save much time and effort
확실하게 전송하다	transfer(send/dispatch) files for sure
빠르고 확실하게	quickly and reliably
어디서나 언제든지	anyplace and anytime/anytime, anywhere
시간과 장소에 상관없이	regardless of(without reference to) time and place
~에 접근하다	access(have access to/get access to)+Ⓝ
쉽게 이용할 수 있는(가능한)	readily(easily) available
잘(더 잘/최상으로) 이용하다	make good(better/the best) use of~
A가 B 하는 것이 가능하다	allow A to B/enable A to B
정보를 얻다	draw(acquire/obtain/get) information
풍부한 자료들	a wealth of materials(resources/references/data)
전자책	electronic books(e-books)
인터넷 응용프로그램	internet application
컴퓨터화	computerization
경쟁 사회에서	in a competitive society
~와 상호작용하다	interact with~
가상의 친구들	virtual friends
무선 통신 기술	wireless technology
컴퓨터 지원 학습 프로그램	computer-assisted(based) learning programs
운영하다/수행하다	conduct/carry out/organize/manage/administer
원격학습	distance learning
과제를 컴퓨터로 제출하다	submit(hand in) assignments on a computer
재택근무	work from home/telecommuting
유용한 도구로서	as a useful(valuable/helpful) tool
인터넷 접속	internet access

인터넷을 검색하다	surf the Internet(web)
때때로	at times/sometimes/once in a while/now and then
한 예로써	for one thing/to cite one example/as an example/to give an example
예를 들어	for instance/for example/to illustrate
더욱이	furthermore/what is more/moreover
이처럼	like this/in this manner/in this regard/in this respect
편리함을 가져오다(야기하다)	result in(lead to/bring about/give rise to) convenience

BODY 2(negative factors)

부정적인 면에서	on the downside/on the negative side/on the minus side
저장된 정보	the information stored/stored information
우연히 삭제되고 모방되다	be deleted and copied by accident(accidentally)
사실을 왜곡하다	distort(strain) the truth(the fact)
표절하다	plagiarize/pirate
무분별한 정보	unreasonable(thoughtless/senseless) information
조작된 정보	fabricated information
개인 정보를 악용하다	make wrong(ill) use of personal information
온라인상에서 명의 도용	identity theft online(on the Internet)
중대한 후유증	grave aftereffect(aftermath)
고통받다	struggle with/suffer from/be sick with/be harassed by
A가 B에 취약하다	A be vulnerable(susceptible) to B
외설적이고 폭력적인 장면	obscene(suggestive) and violent scenes
부정직함, 사기 등과 같은	such as(like/including) dishonesty, fraud and so on
~로 가득 차 있다	teem with/be flooded with~
~에 의해 매료되다	be fascinated by/be entranced by/be attracted by~
부도덕한 짓을 하다	be guilty of immorality/act immorally/commit an immoral act

청소년 비행 문제	the problem of delinquency
컴퓨터 게임에 관하여	with respect to(in light of/in terms of/in the case of) computer games
중독에 대해 걱정하다	be concerned about(be worried about) computer addiction
컴퓨터 게임에 중독되다	be addicted to(be obsessed with) computer games
게임 중독자	a game addict
컴맹	computer illiteracy
공부로부터 집중을 분산시키다	distract attention away from studying
~의 방해를 하다	get (stand) in the way of
VDT증후군/단말기 증후군	VDT(video display terminal) syndrome
젊은이들에게 악영향을 끼치다	have adverse(detrimental/harmful) influences on the youth
~에 적용되다	be applied to+Ⓝ
~에 열중하다	be absorbed in/be glued to/be engrossed in~
~와 관련되다	be associated with/be related to/be connected with/be involved in~
~하는 경향이 있다	be prone to/be liable to/be disposed to/tend to/have a tendency to~
~할 목적으로	with a view to/for the purpose of/with the intention of
~에 유용하지 않다	be of little use(value/benefit) to~
좀처럼 ~않다	hardly/scarcely/seldom/rarely
그러므로	therefore/thus/hence/as a result/in this context

CONCLUSION

결론은	to conclude/In conclusion/to sum up
위에서 언급한 것처럼	as stated above/as mentioned above
A를 고려하다	take A into consideration(account)/take account of A/consider A
필수적인	indispensable/essential/integral/fundamental
엄청난 이점들	immense(tremendous/massive) benefits(strengths)
현명하게	sensibly/wisely/advisably
핵심은	the bottom line is that S+V

SENTENCE PRACTICE

INTRODUCTION

1. 컴퓨터의 출현은 사람들이 다양한 지식을 얻는 방법에 상당한 변화를 가져오고 있다.

_____

_____

2. 이 경향은 주로 이롭지만, 그것에 대한 부정적인 측면이 또한 있다.

_____

_____

3. 이 에세이에서, 학습을 위한 컴퓨터 사용의 장점들과 단점들이 토론될 것이다.

_____

_____

BODY 1

1. 오늘날, 학생들은 컴퓨터로 학습하는 데 드는 시간과 노력을 절약할 수 있다.

_____

_____

2. 그것은 컴퓨터들이 다양한 정보를 제공하는 것 이외에도 과제를 저장하고, 빠르고 확실하게 전송을 가능하게 하기 때문이다.

_____

_____

3. 컴퓨터 이용 이전에는, 학생들은 자료들과 노트를 가지고 다녀야만 했고 그들의 가방이나 선반의 많은 공간을 차지했다.

_____

_____

4. 그뿐만 아니라, 컴퓨터 사용의 이점은 인터넷은 학생들이 쉽게 접근할 수 있는 다양한 강의들과 자료들을 제공한다는 것이다.

_____

_____

5. 요즘은 많은 학교나 교육 기관들이 컴퓨터 지원 학습 프로그램을 수행하고 있어서, 컴퓨터가 유용한 학습 도구로서 필수품이 되고 있다.

---

6. 예를 들면, 많은 대학들은 컴퓨터를 통한 원격학습을 시간과 장소에 상관없이 학생들에게 제공하고 학생들은 또한 과제를 컴퓨터로 제출한다.

---

7. 이처럼, 학습하는 데 유용한 도구가 되는 컴퓨터의 몇 가지 이점들이 있다.

BODY 2

1. 부정적인 면에서 저장된 정보가 우연히 삭제되고 모방되는 경우가 있다.

---

2. 다른 상황에서, 인터넷상의 디지털 자료들은 우연히 또는 의도적으로 표절되고 왜곡될 수 있다.

---

3. 때때로, 이것은 부정직함, 사기 등과 같은 몇 가지 사회문제들을 야기한다.

---

4. 덧붙여서, 인터넷은 무분별하고 쓸모 없는 자료들로 넘쳐나고 있다.

---

5. 만약 학생들이 어떤 정보가 신뢰성이 있는지 구별할 수 없다면, 그들은 그러한 정보에 의해 악영향을 받을 수 있다.

---

6. 다른 단점 요인은 온라인에서 넘쳐나는 오락들이 공부에 집중을 분산시키고 학습을 방해할 수 있다.

_____

_____

7. 이런 관점에서, 컴퓨터는 학습의 도구로서 학생들에게 유용하지 않을 수 있다.

_____

_____

CONCLUSION

1. 요약하자면, 위에서 언급한 것처럼, 학습에 있어서 컴퓨터의 이용은 비록 몇 가지 단점들은 있지만, 더 많은 장점을 가지고 있다.

_____

_____

2. 핵심은 컴퓨터는 학습을 위해서 현명하고 적절하게 이용되어야 한다는 것이다.

_____

_____

ANSWER

INTRODUCTION

1. The advent of computers has made significant changes in the way people acquire a broad range of knowledge.

2. Although this trend is most beneficial, there are also some negative factors for it.

3. In this essay, the pros and cons of using computers for studying will be discussed.

BODY 1

1. Today, students could save much time and effort when studying with computers.

2. It is because computers also enable them to transfer and store files quickly and reliably besides providing various information.

3. Before the use of computers, students had to carry files and notes that took up large spaces in their bags or school lockers.

4. Not only that, the benefits of using a computer are that the Internet provides a wide variety of lectures and materials students can access.

5. Nowadays, as plenty of schools and educational organizations conduct computer-assisted learning programs, computers have become a necessity as a useful educational tool.

6. To illustrate, Distance Learning Courses in universities give lectures and references, regardless of time and place, to students who also submit assignments on a computer.

7. Like this, there are a few good points of computers that make them a useful tool for studying.

BODY 2

1. On the downside, there are occasions when the information stored can be deleted and copied by accident.

2. In other situations, digital information on the Internet can be plagiarized and distorted accidentally or intentionally.

3. At times, this gives rise to a few social problems such as dishonesty, fraud and so on.

4. Moreover, the Internet teems with unreasonable and useless information.

5. Provided that students cannot tell which information is reliable, they could be adversely affected by such information.

6. Another minus factor is that the flood of entertainment online could distract attention away from studying and got in the way of learning.

7. In this respect, computers can be of little use to students as an educational device.

CONCLUSION

1. To sum up, as stated above, the use of computers in studying, although having some drawbacks, has much more strengths.

2. The bottom line is that computers should be utilized wisely and appropriately for studying.

PREVIOUS TEST

1. Maintaining public libraries is a waste of money since computer technology is now replacing their functions. To what extent do you agree or disagree? (2018.)

2. People are considerably on computers. These machines are used in business, medical care and, even crime. What areas will they be used for in the future?

3. Students in schools and universities learn far more from lessons with their teachers compared to other sources, such as television or the internet. Do you agree or disagree? (2018.)

** 첨삭은 **ieltseasywriting.com**

Nuclear technology provided clean, efficient energy, while it also poses a threat to world peace. What are its advantages and disadvantages?

ESSENTIAL VOCA

INTRODUCTION

최근에	in recent years/in recent times/recently
핵 기술	nuclear technology
긴급하고 사회적인 문제	a pressing and social problem(concern/issue/matter/trouble)
많은/다수의 위험	plenty of(a number of/a slew of/a lot of) perils(threats/dangers/risks)
논쟁을 일으키다	spark(trigger/provoke/set off/arise) a controversy(debate/argument)
잘 알려진 사실이다	it is a well-known fact that(it is common knowledge that) S+V
~에 반대하다	be opposed to(be against/lean against/be not in favor of)+Ⓝ
대체 에너지원/재생 에너지	an alternative power source/renewable energy
~에게 중대한 위협을 가하다	pose grave threats to(threaten/pose serious risks to)+Ⓝ
장단점들	pros and cons/advantages and disadvantages/merits and demerits/strengths and weaknesses
자세히 설명하다	spell out/elaborate on/explain in full detail

BODY 1(positive factors)

한편으로는	on the one hand/meanwhile
~의 경우	in the case of/In terms of/when it comes to/in light of~
기술 혁신 덕택으로	with the help of technological innovation/thanks to technological innovation
잘 이용하다	make good use of/employ(exploit) well
필수적인	indispensable/essential/integral/fundamental
환경적이고 깨끗한 에너지나 서비스를 공급하는 기술	green technology
전통적인 에너지 자원	conventional(traditional) energy sources
화석 연료와 비교하여	compared to(in comparison with/as compared with) fossil fuels
핵발전소	a nuclear station/a nuclear power plant
합리적인 가격에	at a reasonable(affordable) cost
엄청난 돈을 절약하다	save(large sums of money/great amounts of money/tons of money)
생산성을 높이다	raise(increase/promote) productivity
연구에 따르면	according to research
의료	medical treatment(service)
고치기 어려운 질병	an incurable disease(illness)
방사선 치료를 받다	undergo(receive) radiation treatment/radiotherapy
의학적 치료로써 도움을 받다	benefit from medical treatment
빠르고 확실하게	quickly and reliably
가치 있는	priceless/valuable/of value
정밀한/정교한	sophisticated/delicate/elaborate
~에 적응하다	get adjusted to/adjust(adapt) to+Ⓝ
~에 익숙하다	get(be) accustomed to/get(be) used to+Ⓝ
~에 유익하다/도움이 되다	be of benefit to/be of help to+Ⓝ
이런 관점에서	in this respect/in this sense/in this light/in this regard
대신하여	on behalf of/in place of
특히	in particular/particularly/specially/notably
그뿐만 아니라	in addition to that/on top of that/not only that

그러므로/따라서	thus/therefore/hence/as a result/in this context/consequently
~에 긍정적인 영향을 끼치다	have positive(affirmative/beneficial) effects(influences/impacts) on~
중요한 영향을 미치다	have important(major) implications for

BODY 2(negative factors)

그와는 반대로	on the contrary/on the other hand/on the flip side
사실상	in fact/as a matter of fact/actually/in reality/virtually
부정적인 측면은	on the downside/on the negative(minus) side
엄청난 위험을 가져오다	bring immense(tremendous/massive) perils
핵무기제조	the manufacture of nuclear weapons
핵발전소들의 폭발	the explosion of nuclear stations(plants)
폭발하다	blow up/detonate/go off/explode
핵실험을 하다	conduct(perform/carry out/do) nuclear tests
방사선 누출에 대해 걱정하다	be concerned about(be worried about) a radiation leak(leakage)
방출하다	give off/emit/discharge/release
독성물질	toxic substances/poisonous matters/toxic materials
~에 치명적이다	be lethal(fatal/deadly) to~
유용하지 않다	be of little use/be useless/be valueless/be of little value
악용하다	make bad(ill) use of/abuse
해로운	detrimental/harmful/pernicious/injurious
쓸모 없는	obsolete/useless/good for nothing
기술적 결함	technical imperfection(deficiency/flaw/defection)
고장 나다	break down/go wrong/be out of order
무분별한	indiscriminate/thoughtless/indiscreet
유해 화학 물질	harmful chemical substances
폐연료 재처리	spent fuel reprocessing
원자폭탄으로 폭격당하다	be bombed with atomic bomb(A-bomb)

그 재난의 여파로	in the wake of the disaster/in the aftermath of the disaster
~에 큰 타격을 주다/큰 피해를 주다	take a toll on~/wreck havoc on~
~에 상당한 영향을 끼치다	have an immense(significant/considerable) impact(influence/effect) on~
A를 위태롭게 하다	endanger A/threaten A/put(place) A in danger
사상자의 수	the toll of casualties(dead and injured)
많은 증상으로 고통받다	struggle with(suffer from/be sick with) symptoms
~에 노출되다	be exposed to(be revealed to/be disclosed to/get exposure to)+Ⓝ
방사능 오염으로 가득 차 있다	be flooded with(overflow with) radioactive contamination(pollution)
광범위하게 미치는 영향	a far-reaching(extensive/far-flung) effect(influence)
곤란에 처하다	be(get) in trouble/be(get) in predicament
어려움에 대처하다	cope with(deal with/handle) difficulties(troubles/hardships)
~의 근처에/주변에	in the vicinity of~/on the periphery of~
주변 환경	surroundings/surrounding environment/environment
야기하다/초래하다	trigger/cause/generate/incur/provoke/induce
초래하다/야기하다	result in(give rise to/bring about/lead to)+Ⓝ
수많은 상황들	countless(numberless) situations(circumstances/conditions)
~의 영향을 받다	be influenced by/be affected by/be under the influence of~
한 예로써	for one thing/to cite one example/as an example
수년 동안	for ages/for years
좀처럼 ~않다	hardly/scarcely/seldom/rarely
못하게 하다	discourage/deter/prevent/dissuade
이로써/이처럼	with this/like this/in this manner/in this regard
~에 해로운 영향을 주다	have harmful(detrimental/adverse/pernicious/negative) influences(impacts/effects) on~

CONCLUSION

결론은	in conclusion/to conclude/in short/to sum up
위에서 언급한 것처럼	as stated above/as mentioned above
~을 이용하다/활용하다	take advantage of/make use of/employ/tap into/exploit
동시에	at the same time/at once/simultaneously/at a time
~에게 위험하다	be dangerous(harmful/hazardous/risky/perilous/precarious) to~
또한	as well/too/likewise/also
관련된 사람들	individuals(people) involved
적절하고 현명하게	reasonably and wisely/properly and rationally/appropriately and sensibly
단점이 장점보다 우세하다	the disadvantages outweigh the advantages
유익한	beneficial/constructive/valuable/advantageous

SENTENCE PRACTICE

INTRODUCTION

1. 최근에 핵 기술은 많은 논쟁들을 일으키고 있다.

_____

_____

2. 핵 기술이 깨끗하고 효율적이기 때문에 좋은 대체 에너지원일 수 있다는 것은 잘 알려진 사실이다.

_____

_____

3. 그러나, 핵 기술의 보유는 또한 인류에게 중대한 위협이 되고 있다.

_____

_____

4. 이 에세이는 핵 기술의 장단점을 자세히 설명할 것이다.

_____

_____

BODY 1

1. 한편으로는, 핵 기술은 몇 가지 장점들이 있다.

_____

_____

2. 그들 중 하나는 질병을 치료하는 데 잘 이용되고 있다는 것이다.

_____

_____

3. 핵 기술이 덕택으로, 환자들은 더 빠르고 효율적으로 의료적 도움을 받을 수 있다.

_____

_____

4. 연구에 따르면, 오늘날 병원들에서 사용되고 있는 모든 치료의 1/3은 방사선을 포함한다.

_____

_____

5. 그뿐만 아니라, 핵 에너지는 화석연료들과 같은 전통적인 에너지 자원과 비교하여 저렴하고 깨끗한 에너지를 공급할 수 있다.

_____

_____

6. 따라서, 많은 나라가 에너지 자원과 의학적 치료로써 도움을 받기 때문에 핵 에너지는 필요하다.

_____

_____

BODY 2

1. 다른 한편으로는, 핵 기술은 핵 발전소와 핵무기에 의해 발생하는 엄청난 위험을 가져올 수 있다.

_____

_____

2. 핵 발전소들의 폭발과 같은 재해들이 있어 왔다.

_____

_____

3. 이러한 것 때문에 거대한 지역이 황폐화되고 많은 사람들이 다쳤다. 그 결과 영향을 받은 이들은 많은 증상들로 힘겨워하고 있다.

_____

_____

4. 예를 들어, 2010년에, 쓰나미가 일본 원자력 발전소 중의 하나를 덮쳤다.

_____

_____

5. 그 재난의 여파로, 원자력 발전소로부터 방사능 유출이 발생했고 이러한 것은 일본뿐만 아니라 주변 국가들에게 큰 타격을 주었다.

_____

_____

6. 더욱이 핵무기를 제조하는 데 이용되고 있다. 이것은 인간에게 치명적이다.

_____

_____

7. 한 가지 예로, 일본이 1945년 원자 폭탄 폭격을 당했을 때, 사상자 수는 상당했다.

_____

_____

8. 최근에는 북한이 핵 실험을 시행하고 있다고 보고되었다.

_____

_____

9. 이것은 한반도뿐만 아니라 세계 전역의 평화를 위협한다.

_____

_____

10. 이처럼 핵 기술은 인간에게 치명적인 무기가 될 수 있다.

_____

_____

CONCLUSION

1. 결론적으로, 위에서 언급된 것처럼, 핵 기술은 몇 가지 이점들이 있다.

_____

_____

2. 동시에, 그것은 사람들이나 환경에 또한 위험하다.

_____

_____

3. 따라서, 만약 국가들과 관련된 사람들이 실용적인 자원으로써 현명하게 그리고 합리적으로 활용한다면 유용할 수 있다.

_____

_____

ANSWER

INTRODUCTION

1. In recent years, nuclear technology has sparked a lot of controversies.

2. It is a well-known fact that nuclear technology can be a good alternative power source since it is clean and efficient.

3. However, the possession of nuclear technology also poses grave threats to humanity.

4. This essay will spell out the advantages and disadvantages of nuclear technology.

BODY 1

1. On the one hand, nuclear technology has several merits.

2. One of them is that it has been made good use of treating diseases.

3. With the help of nuclear technology, patients can receive medical help more quickly and efficiently.

4. According to research, today a third of all procedures used in hospitals involve radiation.

5. In addition to that, nuclear energy is also able to provide cheap and clean energy compared to the conventional energy sources, including fossil fuels.

6. Thus, nuclear power is necessary because many nations benefit from clean power sources and medical treatments.

BODY 2

1. On the other hand, nuclear technology can also bring immense perils caused by nuclear power plants and weapons.

2. There have been disasters such as the explosion of nuclear power stations.

3. Because of which large regions were devastated, and a great number of people were hurt. As a result, those affected struggle with many symptoms.

4. For example, in the year 2010, a tsunami struck one of Japan's power plants.

5. In the wake of the disaster, a radiation leak from a nuclear plant occurred, which took a toll on the neighboring countries as well as Japan.

6. Furthermore, nuclear technology has been utilized in the manufacture of nuclear weapons, which arc lethal to human beings.

7. For one thing, when Japan was bombed with atomic bombs in 1945, the toll of dead and injured was considerable.

8. Recently, it is reported that North Korea has conducted nuclear tests.

9. It threatens peace not only in the Korean peninsula but in the entire world.

10. With this, nuclear technology can be deadly weapons to humans.

CONCLUSION

1. In conclusion, as mentioned above, nuclear technology has several benefits.

2. At the same time, it is dangerous to people and the environment as well.

3. Consequently, if nations and individuals involved take advantage of it wisely and reasonably as a practical resource, it can be beneficial.

PREVIOUS TEST

1. Do you support that the nuclear technology should be used for constructive purposes? Give reasons for your viewpoint.

2. To what extent is nuclear technology a danger to life on Earth? What are the benefits and risks associated with its use?

3. The use of nuclear technology should be discouraged even for civil purposes.
   What is your opinion?

** 첨삭은 ieltseasywriting.com

Education

1. Co-ed school

2. Physical punishment

3. Studying English

4. Teenager's job

5. Practical skill in University

1. Co-ed school

> Some people think that it is better to educate boys and girls in separate schools. Others, however, believe that boys and girls benefit more from attending mixed schools. Discuss both views and give your own opinion.

ESSENTIAL VOCA

INTRODUCTION

학교의 유형에 대한 논란	the controversy(debate) over the type of schooling(school education)
학교 교육	schooling/school education
남녀공학	a co-ed school/a school for both genders/a coeducational school/a mixed school
남녀공학에 비교해서	compared to(in comparison with/as compared with) co-ed schools
남학교/여학교	single-sex schools/schools for either boys or girls
계속되어 온 문제	an ongoing(a continual/a lasting) issue
그러나	however/on the other hand/having said that
분리하다	separate/divide
단점들	demerits/bad points/disadvantages/drawbacks
장점들	metis/good points/advantages/benefits
내 의견으로는	in my opinion/from my point of view
~에 찬성하다	be for/agree with/prefer/be in favor of~
~에 반대하다	be against/disagree with/be not in favor of~
다음과 같이	as follows

BODY 1(the disadvantage of co-ed schools)

우선	first of all/to begin with/above all
관련해서	concerning/with relation to/regarding/as regards/as respects
사실상	as a matter of fact/in fact/virtually/actually
남학생과 여학생들	male and female students/girl and boy students
몇몇의 학생들	a handful of(several/a few/a couple of) students(pupils)
많은 학생들	a number of(a slew of/the majority of the/plenty of) students(pupils)
청소년기에	in adolescence/in an adolescent period
다른 성별과 접촉하다	contact with(make contact with/come in touch with) the opposite gender
이성에 집착하다	be obsessed with(adhere to/stick to) opposite sex(gender)
이성에 반하다	have(has) a crush on the other gender
이성에게 매력을 느끼다	feel attracted to(have an affinity for/feel drawn(attraction) to) the opposite sex
면학 분위기	academic(learning) atmosphere(environment)
수업에 집중할 수가 없다	cannot concentrate on(focus on/pay attention to) classes
공부를 방해하다	impede(hamper/hinder/prevent) study
학업에서 뒤처지다	fall behind(lay behind) with study(school work)
연구에 따르면	according to research(studies)
학업 성적	scholastic(academic) performance(grade/achievement/mark/result)/school record/schoolwork
수업에 참여하다	attend a class/take a course(class)
성적을 향상시킬 수 없다	cannot make progress in academic achievement
새로운 환경에 적응하는 데 두렵다	be afraid of adjusting(adapting) to new environment
~에게 부담이 되다	become a burden to(on)~
취약한/영향받기 쉬운	vulnerable/sensitive/susceptible
스트레스를 받다	get(feel) stressed/stress out/be under stress/suffer from stress
안 좋은 경험들을 겪다	undergo(suffer from/go through) bad(unpleasant/terrible/unfavorable) experiences
문제에 직면하다	face(confront/encounter) problems(difficulties/concerns/troubles)
그 외에도	in addition to that/on top of that/not only that
다시 말해서	in other words/that is to say/namely/to put it another way

~에 부정적인 영향을 끼치다   have a negative(detrimental/harmful/pernicious) influence(effect/impacts) on~

BODY 2(advantages of co-ed schools)

반면에	on the flip side/on the other hand/on the contrary/in contrast/by contrast
성별에 관계없이	regardless of(without reference to) gender
중요한 단계	a key(vital/significant/crucial/critical) step
인격 형성기	the formative years(period)
또래 집단	a peer group
성인기	adulthood/adult period(life)
다양한 경험	a broad(wide) range(variety) of experience
풍부한 지식과 정보	a wealth of knowledge and information
~에게 지식을 전하다	disseminate(impart/convey/delivery) knowledge to~
의견과 생각을 공유하다	share ideas and opinions
학교 친구들과 어울리고 대화하다	mingle and converse(communicate) with schoolchildren
정서적(심적) 그리고 신체적 발달	emotional(mental/psychological) and physical development
신체적·정신적 건강	physical and mental well-being(health)
전인교육	an all-round(a whole-person/a holistic) education
경험을 바탕으로/기본으로	based on experiences
기회들	occasions/opportunities/chances
보람 있는 경험	a rewarding(desirable) experience
사회생활에 적응하다	adapt(adjust) to a social life
사회생활에 많이 기여하다	contribute a great deal to(make a considerable contribution to) a social life
성인기를 준비하다	gear up for(prepare for/be ready for/make preparation for) adult life
학교를 졸업하다	graduate from school/complete school course/finish school
졸업생들	graduates/alumni
가치 있는 직업	a decent(valuable/desirable) job(occupation/profession)
~할 여력이 있다	be capable of/can afford to~

~하는 경향이 있다	be inclined to/tend to/be liable to/have a tendency to~
앞으로/가까운 장래에	down the road/in the near(foreseeable) future
능력을 이용하다	exploit(harness/tap into/make use of/take advantage of) abilities
대단한 도움이 되다	be a great help/be a good help
훨씬 더 ~할 것 같다	be far(much) more likely to~
이러한 맥락에서/따라서	in this context/thus/therefore/as a result/consequently/hence
전반적인 성장을 발전시키다	develop(stimulate/enhance/foster) overall growth
~에 상당한 영향을 끼치다	have(exert) a great(considerable/significant) effect(influence/impact) on~
~에 긍정적인 영향을 끼치다	have(exert) a positive(affirmative/beneficial) impact(influence/effect) on~

CONCLUSION

요약하자면	to sum up/in conclusion/to conclude
위에서 언급한 것처럼	as mentioned above/as stated above
~라는 사실에도 불구하고	despite the fact that S+V
이러한 상황으로 볼 때	given this situation/given these circumstances
이점들이 불리한 점들보다 훨씬 크다	the advantages far(greatly) outweigh the disadvantages
분명히/확실히	definitely/surely/clearly/absolutely/for sure
활성화시키다	promote/expand/increase/support/encourage
설득력 있는	compelling/convincing/persuasive

SENTENCE PRACTICE

INTRODUCTION

1. 학교 교육의 유형에 대한 논란이 계속되어 오고 있다.

_____

_____

2. 일부의 부모들과 선생님들은 남녀공학에서 공부하는 것은 학생들에게 더 도움이 된다고 믿는다.

_____

_____

3. 그러나, 다른 사람들은 남학생과 여학생을 분리시키고 그들을 다른 학교에서 교육시키는 것을 찬성한다.

_____

_____

4. 내 의견으로는, 두 견해는 장단점을 가지고 있다.

_____

_____

5. 이 에세이는 다음과 같이 이 문제에 대해서 논의할 것이다.

_____

_____

BODY 1

1. 남학생과 여학생을 분리하는 데는 몇 가지 이점들이 있다.

_____

_____

2. 우선 단일 성별 학교에서의 학생들은 그들의 공부에 집중할 수 있다.

_____

_____

3. 사실상 학생들이 청소년기에 서로 관심을 가지는 것은 아주 당연하다.

_____

_____

4. 이러한 상황은 학생들을 공부에서 멀어지게 할 수 있고 학교 생활에 지장을 줄 수 있다.

_____

_____

5. 예를 들어, 반 여학생에게 반한 남학생은 그들의 공부 대신에 청소년기의 연애 감정에 집중할 수 있다.

_____

_____

6. 연구에 따르면, 단일 학교 학생의 성적이 남녀 공학에 다니는 학생보다 훨씬 낫다고 한다.

_____

_____

7. 따라서, 남녀 학생들을 분리함으로써 면학 분위기가 학생들을 위해서 만들어질 수 있고 거기에서 그들은 그들의 학업에 훨씬 더 집중할 수 있다.

_____

_____

BODY 2

1. 반면에, 남학생들과 여학생들이 다른 학교에서 공부하는 것은 몇 가지 문제에 또한 마주친다.

_____

_____

2. 단일 성별 학교는 학생들이 이성과 교류할 기회를 제공하지 못한다.

_____

_____

3. 그 결과, 졸업생들은 사회생활에서 서로 의견과 생각을 나누는 것이 어렵다는 것을 발견한다.

_____

_____

4. 사실상, 아이들의 인격 형성기는 성별과 관계없이 어떻게 어울리고 대화하는지에 대해 배우고 성인의 삶을 준비하는 최상의 시기이다.

_____

_____

5. 이러한 점에서, 남녀공학은 학생들이 다양한 주제에 대한 그들의 관점을 함께 교류하도록 많은 기회를 제공한다.

_____

_____

6. 이것은 앞으로 학생들이 사회생활에 적응하도록 유도한다.

_____

_____

CONCLUSION

1. 요약하자면, 남녀공학과 단일 성별 학교들은 장점들과 단점들을 가지고 있다.

_____

_____

2. 나의 의견은, 그렇지만, 남녀공학의 장점들이 단점들을 훨씬 능가한다고 생각한다.

_____

_____

3. 이러한 상황으로 볼 때, 부모들과 선생님들이 남녀공학의 교육을 활성화시키는 것이 설득력이 있다.

_____

_____

ANSWER

INTRODUCTION

1. The controversy over the type of schooling has been an ongoing issue.

2. Some parents and teachers believe that attending co-ed schools is more beneficial for schoolchildren.

3. Others, having said that, are for separating boys and girls.

4. In my opinion, both views have merits and demerits.

5. This essay will discuss this issue as follows.

BODY 1

1. There are some benefits to separating male and female students.

2. First of all, students in single-sex schools could concentrate on their study.

3. It is quite natural for students in adolescence to feel attracted to each other.

4. This circumstance could lead students to distract studying and interfere with social life.

5. For example, boys who have a crush on a female classmate could focus on adolescent romances instead of their study.

6. According to research, school records single-sex schools are much better than those in co-ed schools.

7. Therefore, by separating boys and girls, an academic atmosphere can be created for students in which they could pay far more attention to their learning.

BODY 2

1. On the flip side, boys and girls studying in different schools encounter some problems as well.

2. Single-sex schools do not provide an opportunity for students to interact with the other gender.

3. As a result, graduates find it difficult to share ideas and opinions with each other in their social life.

4. In reality, the formative years of children are the best time to learn more about how to mingle and converse with schoolchildren regardless of gender to gear up for adult life.

5. In this respect, co-ed schools offer many chances for students to exchange their points of views on various subjects together

6. , which cause children to adapt to their social life down the road.

CONCLUSION

1. To sum up, co-ed schools and single-sex schools have their merits and demerits.

2. In my opinion, the advantages of co-ed schools far outweigh the disadvantages, though.

3. Given this situation, it is compelling for parents and teachers to promote mixed school education.

PREVIOUS TEST

1. Some people think that they can learn better by themselves than with a teacher. Others think that it is always better to have a teacher. Which do you prefer?

2. Some people say that education system is the only critical factor to the development of a country. To what extent do you agree or disagree with this statement?

3. All education(primary, secondary and further education) should be free to all people and paid and managed by the government.
Do you agree or disagree with this statement?

** 첨삭은 ieltseasywriting.com

2. Physical punishment

Some parents say corporal punishment, at times, is necessary to educate children. They state that the benefits of this punishment far outweigh the demerits. What is your opinion?

ESSENTIAL VOCA

INTRODUCTION

체벌	physical(corporal) punishment
~에 체벌을 가하다	impose(inflict/delivery) punishment on/dole out corporal punishment to~
훈육하다/지도하다	discipline/educate/instruct
잘못된 행동	wrong behavior/wrong-doing/misdeed/misconduct
~하는 경향이 있다	have a tendency to/tend to/be inclined to/be liable to~
계속되어 온 문제	an ongoing(continual/lasting) issue
~에 대한 논란	a controversy(debate) over~
효과에 대해 의문을 제기하다	raise the question of the effects
훈육과 관련해서	concerning(regarding/as regards) discipline
내 경우에는	as for me/in my case/from my point of view
때때로	occasionally/at times/once in a while/now and then
~에 반대하다	be against(disagree with/be not in favor of)+Ⓝ
그 의견에 찬성한다	be for(be in favor of/agree with/support) the idea
자세히 설명하다	elaborate on/spell out/explain in full detail
다음의 의견들은 그 이유들이다	the following arguments are the reasons

BODY 1(disagree)

우선	to begin with/first of all/above all
부정적인 요인들	negative factors(causes/influences/aspects/parts)
체벌에 취약하다	be vulnerable(sensitive/susceptible) to physical punishment
정서적 그리고 신체적 발달(건강)	emotional and physical development(well-being/health)
연약한 정신과 신체에 손상을 주다	damage(ravage/injure/hurt) fragile mind and body
아이들의 정서적 성장을 방해하다	impede(hamper/hinder/prevent) children's emotional growth
체벌 때문에	due to(because of/owing to/on account of) physical punishment
자살하다	kill oneself/commit suicide
~에 좌절하다	be(get/feel) frustrated at/feel(get) discouraged by/feel(get) disheartened at~
우울증	depression/the blues(구어체)
상처	a wound/an injury/a bruise
힘든 상황	desperate(harsh/terrible) circumstances
스트레스를 받다	get(feel) stressed/stress out/be under stress/suffer from stress
~에 자신감을 갖지 못하다	have no confidence in~
자신감의 부족을 느끼다	feel a lack of confidence
A가 B 하는 것을 막다	prevent(deter/stop/prohibit/inhibit) A from B
~하는 데 어려움을 겪다	have difficulty(trouble) in ~ing
안 좋은 경험들을 겪다	undergo(suffer from/go through) bad(unpleasant/unfavorable) experiences
극복할 수 없는 어려움	insuperable difficulties(troubles/concerns)
문제에 직면하다	face(confront/encounter) problems
체벌에 익숙하다	be used to(get used to/get accustomed to) corporal punishment
잘못된 개념을 주다	give children the wrong idea(conception)
사람이 실수를 저지르는 한	so long as people make a mistake
그러한 폭력은 용납되다	such violence is acceptable
체벌을 당연한 것으로 여기다	take physical punishment for granted
악순환	a vicious cycle(circle)
가까운 미래에	down the road/in the near(foreseeable) future

| 다음 세대에 물려주다 | pass to the next generation |
| ~에 해로운 영향을 끼친다 | have(has) detrimental(negative/harmful/pernicious) influences(impacts/effects) on~ |

BODY 2

부작용	a side effect/an adverse reaction
역효과를 낳는	counterproductive
아이들에게 아무 도움이 안 된다	lead children nowhere
거의 도움이 되지 않는다/이익이 되지 않는다	be of little benefit/be of little help
다시 말해서	in other words/that is to say/that is/namely/to put it another way
체벌의 초기의 목적	the initial(desired) purpose(intention/aim) of physical punishment
실수를 바로 잡다	correct(rectify) mistakes
시행착오	trial and error
교육적인 도구/수단	an educational tool(measure/step/way)
주의 사항/따라 할 규칙	dos and don'ts
전인교육	a well-rounded(a whole-rounded/all-rounded) education
중요한 단계	a key(vital/significant/critical) step
연약한	fragile/weak/delicate/feeble
인격 형성기	the formative years/the formative period
성인기	adulthood/adult period/adult life
가정폭력	domestic violence
과보호 부모	overprotective parents
부모의 지도	parental guidance
부모님의 기대에 부응하다	live up to parents' expectations
거짓말하다	tell a lie/tell an untruth
부모님에 대해 부정적인 감정	negative(hard) feelings toward(against) parents
분노로 변한다	turn into resentment(anger/rage/fury/wrath)
~에 집착하다	be obsessed with/adhere to/stick to+Ⓝ

만약 ~이라면	provided(that) S+V
야기하다/초래하다/일으키다	lead to(result in/give rise to/bring about)+Ⓝ
발생시키다/초래하다	prompt/generate/trigger/cause/provoke/incur/induce

CONCLUSION

요약하면	to sum up/in conclusion/to conclude
위에서 언급한 것처럼	as mentioned above/as stated above
이러한 이유들을 감안하면	given that these reasons
단점들	drawbacks/demerits/shortcomings/disadvantages/weaknesses
B만큼 A가 아니다	not as A as B
~에 대한 책임이 있다	have responsibility for/be accountable(responsible) for/be to blame for~
의식을 높이다	raise(heighten/foster/increase) awareness(consciousness)
설득력 있는 해결책	a convincing(persuasive/compelling/valid) solution(approach)
생산적인/효율적인	productive/effective/efficient
훨씬 더 ~할 것 같다	be far(much) more likely to~
분명한	apparent/obvious/clear/evident/clear-cut

SENTENCE PRACTICE

INTRODUCTION

1. 체벌은 아이들을 교육시키는 데 때때로 사용되고 있다.

_____

_____

2. 왜냐하면 많은 부모들은 체벌이 아이들의 잘못된 행동을 바로잡는 데 가장 적절하고 쉬운 방법이라고 믿는 경향이 있기 때문이다.

_____

_____

3. 그러나 어떤 부모들은 훈육과 관련해서 체벌에 대한 효과에 의문을 제기한다.

_____

_____

4. 나로서는, 체벌에 동의하지 않는다.

_____

_____

5. 다음의 의견은 그 이유들이다.

_____

_____

BODY 1

1. 우선 체벌은 아이들의 정서적 그리고 신체적 발달에 해로운 영향을 줄 수 있다.

_____

_____

2. 아이들에게 체벌을 가하는 것은 그들에게 그러한 폭력은 받아들여질 수 있는 것이라는 잘못된 개념을 줄지도 모른다.

_____

_____

3. 이것은 체벌이 잘못된 것을 바로잡는 데 필요하다는 견해를 야기할지도 모른다.

_____

_____

4. 예를 들어, 체벌을 경험한 아이들은 누군가가 실수를 하는 한 체벌하는 것은 이치에 맞는다고 생각한다.

_____

_____

5. 그런 이유로, 그들이 성장한 후에 똑같은 방법으로 그들의 아이들을 체벌하는 경향이 있다.

_____

_____

6. 더욱이, 아이들의 신체는 아직 완전히 발달하지 못했고, 그래서 아직은 정신적, 신체적으로 취약하다.

_____

_____

7. 그러므로, 그들에게 고통을 가하는 것은 연약한 정신과 신체에 손상을 주는 것이다. 그리고 또한 그 상처를 치유하는 데 시간이 걸린다.

_____

_____

8. 이처럼, 폭력의 사용에 의한 처벌은 악순환을 야기할 수 있고 아이들의 신체적, 정신적 건강에 해를 줄 수 있다.

_____

_____

BODY 2

1. 그것 이외에도, 체벌은 아이들에게 아무 도움이 안 된다.

_____

_____

2. 우선, 그들에게 기대된 이로운 효과는 오래 지속하지 못하고 결국 역효과를 낳는다.

_____

_____

3. 사실상, 체벌의 초기 목적인 아이들을 꾸짖고 다시 잘못 행동하는 것을 막는 것은 전혀 성취되지 못할 것이다.

_____

_____

4. 이것에 덧붙여서, 체벌은 아이들이 그들의 잘못을 깨닫도록 허용하지 않는다.

_____

_____

5. 사실상, 이러한 종류의 체벌은 아이들 사이에 두려움을 불러일으키고 체벌을 피하기 위해서 다음에는 거짓말을 유도한다.

_____

_____

6. 더욱이 아이들을 위한 체벌의 교육적 의도는 그들의 부모에 향하는 분노와 다른 부정적으로 감정으로 변할지도 모른다.

_____

_____

7. 따라서, 부모들과 자식들간의 관계는 교육적 도구로서의 체벌 때문에 악화될 수 있다.

_____

_____

CONCLUSION

1. 요약하면, 위에서 언급한 것처럼, 체벌에 몇 가지 단점들이 존재하는 것은 분명하다.

_____

_____

2. 그러한 체벌의 효과는 부모들이 기대한 만큼 교육적이지도 생산적이지도 않다.

_____

_____

3. 그러므로, 부모들이 아이들을 체벌이 아닌 합리적인 방법으로 훈육하는 것이 설득력이 있다.

_____

_____

ANSWER

INTRODUCTION

1. Physical punishment is occasionally used to discipline children

2. since many parents have a tendency to believe it is the most appropriate and easiest way to correct the wrong behavior of their children.

3. However, some raise the question of the effects of physical punishment concerning discipline.

4. As for me, I am not for corporal punishment.

5. The following arguments are the reasons.

BODY 1

1. Above all, corporal punishment could have detrimental effects on children's emotional and physical development.

2. Inflicting corporal punishment on children may give them the wrong idea that such violence is acceptable.

3. This may lead to the view that corporal punishment is necessary to correct wrongdoings.

4. For example, children who experience physical punishment would think doling out corporal punishment to somebody is reasonable so long as they have made a mistake.

5. On that account, after they grow up, they would tend to punish their children in the same way.

6. Moreover, children are not yet fully developed, and hence they are still vulnerable mentally and physically.

7. Therefore, imposing pain upon them might damage their fragile mind and body, and it also takes a long time for the wounds to heal.

8. In this way, punishment by the use of violence could result in a vicious cycle and could harm children's physical well-being.

BODY 2

1. On top of that, physical punishment leads children nowhere.

2. To begin with, the expected beneficial effect on it does not last long and is ultimately counterproductive.

3. In fact, the initial purpose of physical punishment, which is to scold children and prevent him or her from misconduct, would not be achieved at all.

4. In addition to that, physical punishment does not allow children to realize what they have done wrong.

5. In reality, this kind of penalty only causes fear among children that may prompt them to tell a lie next time to avoid the punishment.

6. Moreover, the educational intention of physical punishment for education may turn into resentment and other negative feelings toward their patents.

7. As a result, the relationship between parents and children could become worse due to physical punishment as an educational tool.

CONCLUSION

1. To sum up, as mentioned above, it is apparent that some drawbacks of corporal punishment exist.

2. The effect of such a kind of punishment is not as educational and productive as patents expect.

3. Therefore, it is convincing for parents to discipline children in sensible ways, but not with physical punishment.

PREVIOUS TEST

1. Some people say that the government should decide what subjects a student can study, while others believe that the students should decide what they want to study. Discuss both views and give your opinion. (2018. 02.)

2. It is important for children to learn the difference between right and wrong at an early age. Punishment is necessary to help them learn this distinction. To what extent do you agree or disagree with this opinion?

3. Discipline is an ever-increasing problem in modern schools. Some people think that discipline should be the responsibility of teachers, while others think that this is the role of parents. Discuss both sides and give your opinion.

** 첨삭은 **ieltseasywriting.com**

Some people believe that studying English in an English-speaking country is the best way to learn the language. What is your opinion?

ESSENTIAL VOCA

INTRODUCTION

최근에	in recent years/in recent times/recently
잘 알려진 사실이다	it is a well-known fact that S+V
보편적인/국제적인 언어	a universal(international/global) language/lingua franca
영어권 나라들	English-speaking countries(nations)/the English-speaking world
세계적인 추세	a global(worldwide) trend
그런 이유 때문에/그래서	accordingly/for this(that) reason/on that account
~하기를 간절히 원하다	be keen to/be anxious to/be dying to/be eager to~
가장 효율적인 방법	the most efficient(successful/useful/helpful) way
언어 구사 능력	language skills(abilities)/a command of the language
부정적인 요인들	negative factors(causes/influences/aspects/parts)
단점들	demerits/bad points/disadvantages/drawbacks
~에 반대하다	be against(disagree with/be not in favor of)+Ⓝ
그 의견에 찬성한다	be for(be in favor of/agree with/support) the idea
주장하다	argue/maintain/state/stress/believe/claim
이것과 관련해서	in this regard/in this manner/in this respect
자세히 설명하다	elaborate on/spell out/explain in full detail

BODY 1(agree)

한편으로는	on the one hand/meanwhile
분명한	clear-cut/clear/apparent/obvious
영어를 사용하는 환경	an English-language environment(surroundings)
매일의 상황에서	on day-to-day situations/in daily circumstances
영어권 문화에 친숙하다	be familiar with English culture
영어 환경에 노출되다	be exposed to(get exposure to) an English environment(surroundings/circumstances)
~을 하기 위한 많은 기회를 갖는다	get(gain/have) a lot of opportunities(experiences/chances) to~
언어기술의 빠른 발전	the rapid development of language skills
다양한 경험	a wide(broad/whole) range(variety) of experiences
이국적 문화에 적응하다	adapt to(adjust to) exotic culture
익숙해지다	get(become) accustomed to+Ⓝ/get(become) used to+Ⓝ
더 나은 문화 이해	a better understanding of culture
예를 들어	to give an illustration/for instance/for example
홈 스테이 프로그램	a homestay program
생활양식을 이해하다	understand the lifestyle
대화 기술을 발전시키다	develop(improve) communication skills
풍부한 지식과 정보	a wealth of knowledge and information
성취감	a sense of achievement/a sense of accomplishment
가치 있는 직업	a decent(desirable) job(occupation/profession)
경험을 바탕으로/기본으로	based on experiences
보람 있는 경험	a rewarding experience
능력을 이용하다	exploit(make use of/take advantage of/use) abilities
대단한 도움이 되다	be a great help/be greatly(very) helpful
대단히 노력하다	make considerable(great) efforts
많이 기여하다	contribute a great deal to(make an considerable contribution to)+Ⓝ
A가 B 하는 것을 허락하다(가능하게 하다)	allow A to B/enable A to B
원어민과 어울리고 대화하다	mingle and converse(communicate) with natives(local people)

외국에서 공부하기를 열렬히 원하다	be keen to(be eager to/be anxious to) study overseas(abroad)
언어를 습득하다	acquire(learn) languages
영어를 잘하다	have a good command of(be proficient in/be good at) English
부인할 수 없다	It cannot be denied that(there is no denying that) S+V
그런 이유 때문에	accordingly/for this reason/on that account
~에 긍정적인 영향을 끼치다	have a positive(affirmative/beneficial) impact(influence/effect) on~
일반적이다	It is not uncommon that S+V

BODY 2(disagree)

다른 한편으로는	on the flip side/on the other hand/on the contrary
~와 비교하여	compared to/in comparison with/as compared with
A에게 아무 도움이 안 된다/효과가 없다	lead A nowhere
~에 부정적인 영향을 끼치다	have(has) a negative(detrimental/harmful/pernicious) influence on~
사실상	as a matter of fact/in fact/virtually/actually
다양한 자료들	a range of(a variety of) materials(sources/references)
어려운(힘든) 경험	a daunting(challenging/demanding/harsh) experience
외국 환경	exotic surroundings/a foreign environment
언어적이고 문화적인 장벽	linguistic and cultural barriers(obstacles)
안 좋은 경험들을 겪다	undergo(suffer from/go through) unpleasant(bitter) experiences
익숙하지 않은 주변환경에 취약하다	be vulnerable(susceptible/sensitive) to unfamiliar surroundings(environment/circumstances)
새로운 환경에 적응하는 것을 두려워하다	be afraid of adjusting(adapting) to a new environment
스트레스를 받다	get(feel) stressed/stress out/be under stress/suffer from stress
대처하다	cope with/deal with/handle
이러한 이유들을 감안하면	given that these reasons
외국에서 공부하는 비용	the cost of studying abroad(overseas)
~에게 부담이 되다	become a burden to(on)+Ⓝ
해외에 머무르는 비용	the cost of staying overseas(abroad)

무거운 재정적인 부담	a heavy financial load(burden/responsibility/obligation)
비용 절감	cost savings/cost cutting/reduction in expenses
역효과를 낳은(비생산적인)	counterproductive(nonproductive/unproductive)
향수병	homesickness(nostalgia)
불안과 우울증	anxiety and depression
극복할 수 없는 어려움(걱정)	insuperable difficulties(troubles/worries/problems)
방해하다	impede/hamper/hinder/prevent
문제없이/원활하게	without any hitches/without any troubles(problems/difficulties/concerns)
~을 야기하다	lead to(result in/give rise to/bring about)+Ⓝ
~라는 사실에도 불구하고	despite the fact that S+V
이런 점에서	In this respect/in this light/in this regard/like this

CONCLUSION

요약하자면	in conclusion/to conclude/to sum up
위에서 언급한 것처럼	as mentioned above/as stated above
당연하다	It is natural that(it stands to reason that/it is proper that) S+V
B보다 A가 훨씬 중요하다	A far outweigh B
훨씬 더 ~할 것 같다	be far(much) more likely to+V
이러한 상황에서	under these circumstances
어느 정도	to some extent/to some degree/more or less/somewhat
영어 문화에 접근하다	have access to(access) English culture
유익한	beneficial/useful/helpful

SENTENCE PRACTICE

INTRODUCTION

1. 영어가 최근에 보편적인 언어가 되고 있다는 것은 잘 알려진 사실이다.

_____

_____

2. 따라서, 세계 각국의 사람들은 다른 언어들보다 영어를 배우고 싶어 한다.

_____

_____

3. 이것과 관련해서, 어떤 사람들은 언어를 배우는 가장 효과적인 방법은 영어권에서 공부하는 것이라고 주장한다.

_____

_____

4. 그러나, 다른 이들은 이 의견에 반대한다.

_____

_____

5. 이 에세이에서 나는 두 가지 의견을 자세히 설명하겠다.

_____

_____

BODY 1

1. 한편으로는, 영어권 나라에서 영어를 배우는 것이 언어를 습득하는 효율적인 방법이라는 것은 분명하다.

_____

_____

2. 그러한 나라에서 머무름으로써, 국제 학생들은 언어를 말하고 듣는 많은 기회를 가질 수 있는 환경에 더 깊숙이 노출될 수 있다.

_____

_____

3. 이러한 것은 그들의 언어기술의 빠른 발전을 야기할 수 있다.

_____

_____

4. 덧붙여서, 외국 학생들은 영어권 나라들에서 사람들의 생활 양식을 포함한 문화에 친숙해질 수 있다.

_____

_____

5. 이러한 것은 더 나은 문화의 이해와 언어 발달을 초래한다.

_____

_____

6. 예를 들어, 외국에서 홈 스테이 프로그램은 생활양식을 이해하고, 대화기술을 발전시키는 데 좋은 경험이다.

_____

_____

7. 이것을 통해서, 학생들은 홈 스테이 가족과 공동체 그리고 등등과 같은 다른 상황에서 지역민들과 어울릴 수 있다.

_____

_____

8. 그러므로, 영어권 문화에 대한 노출은 언어구상능력을 매우 발전시킬 수 있다.

_____

_____

BODY 2

1. 다른 한편으로는, 영어권 나라에서 영어를 배우는 것은 학생들에게 또한 부정적인 영향을 끼칠 수 있다.

_____

_____

2. 실제로는, 사람들이 그들의 나라에서 영어를 배울 수 있게 하는 다양한 자료들과 학원들이 있다.

_____

_____

3. 그러므로 학생들이 해외에 갈 필요가 없다고 주장되고 있다.

_____

_____

4. 더욱이, 해외에 머무르는 비용은 모국에서 머무르는 것과 비교하여 과도하게 높다.

_____

_____

5. 그것뿐만 아니라, 외국 학생들은 엄청난 언어적이고 문화적인 장벽들에 직면할 수 있다.

_____

_____

6. 이러한 것들 때문에, 그들이 외국 환경에 적응하는 게 힘들다.

_____

_____

7. 어떤 경우에는, 그들은 공부하기 위해서 외국에 머물 때 우울증과 향수병을 경험한다.

_____

_____

8. 따라서, 외국에서 영어를 배우는 것은 어렵고 힘든 도전일 수 있다.

_____

_____

CONCLUSION

1. 요약하자면, 영어권 나라에서 영어를 배우는 것은 장점들과 단점들을 가지고 있다.

_____

_____

2. 내 의견으로는, 비록 부정적인 영향들이 있지만, 영어권에서 영어를 배우는 것은 사람들의 배움에 훨씬 더 많은 유익한 영향을 줄 것 같다.

_____

_____

3. 왜냐하면, 그들은 영어 문화에 직접적으로 접근할 기회들을 가질 것이고 이런 상황에서 더 자주 영어를 사용할 것이기 때문이다.

_____

_____

ANSWER

INTRODUCTION

1. It is a well-known fact that English has become a universal language in recent years.

2. Accordingly, people around the world are keen to learn English more than other languages.

3. In this regard, some people argue that the most efficient way to learn English is to study in the English-speaking world.

4. Others, however, are against this idea.

5. In this essay, I will spell out both ideas.

BODY 1

1. On the one hand, it is clear-cut that learning English in an English-speaking country is an effective way of acquiring the language.

2. By being in such countries, international students could be more deeply exposed to an English environment where they could gain a lot of opportunities to speak and listen to English

3. , which could result in the rapid development of their language skills.

4. In addition to that, international students could be familiar with the culture, including people's lifestyles in English-speaking countries

5. , which could give rise to a better understanding of culture and the development of language.

6. To give an illustration, a homestay program in a foreign country is a great experience to understand the lifestyle and develop their communication skill.

7. From this, learners mingle with the locals in different situations such as homestay families, communities and so on.

8. Therefore, the exposure to an English culture can improve immensely a command of the language.

BODY 2

1. On the other hand, it is believed that learning English in English-speaking countries can have an adverse influence on the students as well.

2. In reality, there are various materials and academics, which allow people to learn English in their country.

3. Thus, it is argued that it is not necessary for students to go abroad.

4. Moreover, the cost of staying overseas is extremely high compared to being in one's native country.

5. Not only that, international students can face immense linguistic and cultural barriers.

6. Due to which it can be hard for them to adjust to exotic surroundings.

7. In some cases, they experience depression and homesickness when they stay abroad to study.

8. Hence, learning English overseas could be a harsh and daunting challenge.

CONCLUSION

1. To sum up, learning English in the English-speaking world has both benefits and drawbacks.

2. In my view, studying English there, although having adverse effects, is far more likely to have beneficial impacts on people's learning.

3. since they would have great opportunities to have direct access to English culture and use English frequently under these circumstances.

PREVIOUS TEST

1. As computers translate quickly and accurately, learning foreign languages is a waste of time? To what extent do you agree or disagree?

2. Scientists predict that all people will choose to talk the same global language in the future. Do you think this is a positive or negative development?

3. Being able to speak foreign languages is an advantage these days. Some people think that children should start learning a foreign language at primary school, while others think children should begin in secondary school. Discuss both sides and give your opinion.

** 첨삭은 ieltseasywriting.com

4. Teenager's job

Recently, teenagers have tended to work while they are still students. Do the advantages of this trend outweigh the disadvantages?

ESSENTIAL VOCA

INTRODUCTION

최근에	in recent years/in recent times/recently
~이 잘 알려진 사실이다	it is a well-known fact that S+V
십대들을 고용하다	employ(hire/take on) teenagers
갭이어(고등학교 졸업 후 대학 진학 전에 1년간 다른 목적으로 휴식을 가지는 해)	a gap year
1년간 휴학하다	take(have) a year off from school
인격 형성기	the formative years/the formative period
성인기	adulthood/adult period/adult life
~에 대비하다(준비하다)	gear up for(prepare for/be ready for/make preparation for)~
중요한 단계	a key(vital/significant/critical/crucial) step
~에 대한 논란	a controversy over/a debate over~
장점들	merits/advantages/good points/benefits
부정적인 요인들	a negative factor(cause/influence/aspect/part)
단점들	demerits/bad points/disadvantages/drawbacks
주장하다	argue/claim/believe/maintain/assert
이것과 관련해서/이런 점에서	in this regard/in this respect/in this relation
~에 대해 부분적으로 동의하다	partially(partly) agree with(approve of/consent to)~

자세히 설명하다	elaborate on/spell out/explain in full detail/give an in-depth account of
다음이 그 몇 가지 이유이다	the following are some of the reasons

BODY 1(disagree)

일반적으로	in general/generally/commonly
학업 성적	scholastic(academic) performances(grades/marks/results)
공부를 게을리하다	neglect study/make little efforts to do schoolwork
공부에 집중할 수 없다	cannot focus on(concentrate on/pay attention to) study
수업에 주의가 산만하다	get distracted during class
더 이상 과제할 시간이 없다	no longer have time to do assignments
학교 생활을 방해하다	interfere with(disturb/interrupt) school life
공부에 뒤처지다	fall behind(lay behind) with study
어려운/힘든 일	a daunting(challenging/demanding/harsh/laborious/tough) task(job)
힘든 경험	a demanding(challenging/harsh) experience
친숙하지 않은 주변 환경	unfamiliar surroundings(environment/circumstances)
스트레스를 받다	get(feel) stressed/stress out/be under stress/suffer from stress
안 좋은 경험들을 겪다	undergo(suffer from/go through) unpleasant(bitter) experiences
새로운 환경에 적응하는 것을 두려워하다	be afraid of adjusting(adapting) to a new environment
문제에 직면하다	face(confront/encounter) problems
피로에 지쳐서 집에 돌아오다	come home with exhaustion
이것에 덧붙여서	in addition to that/on top of that/not only that/additionally
학교 활동에 참가하다	attend(participate in/take part in/get involved in/engage in) school activities
전반적인 성장을 촉진하다	boost(stimulate/promote/develop) overall growth
예를 들어	for instance/for example/to illustrate/to give an illustration
과외활동	extracurricular activities/after-school activities/student activities outside of school hours
우정과 협동심	friendship and cooperation
학교 친구들과 어울리고 대화하다	mingle and converse(communicate) with schoolchildren

이러한 이유들을 감안할 때/고려하면	given that these reasons
이치에 맞다	make sense/be logical/stand to reason
~에 부정적인 영향을 끼치다	have(exert) a negative(detrimental/harmful/pernicious) influence on

BODY 2(agree)

직업을 갖다	hold(have/get) a job/be in work
직업 경험/일 경험	work experience/professional experience
사실상	in fact/as a matter of fact/virtually/actually
다양한 지식과 정보를 얻다	acquire a far-reaching(broad) range of knowledge and information
~할 기회를 갖다	have opportunities(chances/occasions) to~
풍부한 경험	a wealth of(a great deal/rich) experience
보람 있는 경험	a rewarding experience
성취감	a sense of achievement(accomplishment)
경험을 바탕으로/기본으로	based on experience
능력을 이용하다	exploit(make use of/take advantage of/exploit) power(ability/capacity)
사회에서 어울리다	fit in society/socialize
직업적인 기술을 발전시키다	develop(hone/advance) professional skills
직업을 통해 실제 사회에 노출되다	gain(get) exposure to(be exposed to) the real world through a job
사회와 교류하다	have interaction with a society/interact with a society
다양한 사람들과 접촉하다	contact with(come in touch with/keep in touch with) various people
대인관계 기술에 많이 기여하다	contribute a great deal to(make a considerable contribution to) interpersonal skills
직업적인 기술을 연마하다	hone(develop/advance) professional skills
취업난	job crunch/job crisis/unemployment
취업(직업) 전망	job(career) prospects
앞으로/가까운 장래에	down the road/in the near(foreseeable) future
학교를 졸업하다	graduate from school/complete whole courses/finish school
돈을 관리하다	manage(handle/cope with/deal with) money

수업료	tuition fees/school fees/tuition
필요 경비	necessary expenses(costs/outlay/expenditure)
비용을 줄이다	curtail(lessen/lighten/reduce) spending(costs/expenses)
어느 정도	somewhat/to some extent(degree)/more or less
부모님에 대한 재정적 부담	financial burden on the parents
여력이 있다	can afford to/be capable of/have power to
다양한 배경	various backgrounds
~에 대단한 도움이 되다	be of great help to/be greatly(very) helpful to~
전공	major/specialty
~에 대해 결정하다	make a decision about~
추구하다	pursue/seek/look for
그 이후에	following that/after that
~에 긍정적인 영향을 주다	have(exert) positive(affirmative/beneficial) influences(effects) on~

CONCLUSION

결론은	to conclude/in conclusion/to sum up
가치 있는 직업	a decent(desirable) job(occupation/profession)
학기 중에	during the academic year/during the school year
~에게 이익이 되다	be of benefit to/be beneficial to~
스스로	on one's own/for oneself/without assistance
미래에 설계하다	design(plan/project/shape) the future
재정적으로	financially/economically
따라서/그러므로	thus/therefore/consequently/as a result/in this context
해야 한다	should/had better/ought to/be supposed to
A가 B 하는 것을 막다	deter(prevent/prohibit/inhibit) A from B
설득력이 있는	compelling/persuasive/convincing
~에 관심을 갖다	pay attention to/take an interest in/get interested in~

SENTENCE PRACTICE

INTRODUCTION

1. 요즘 일부 회사에서 학교에 다니는 십대들을 고용하고 있는 것은 잘 알려진 사실이다.

_____

_____

2. 이것과 관련해서, 어떤 사람들은 직업을 갖는 것은 십대들이 그들의 성인기를 대비하기 위해서 중요한 단계라고 주장한다.

_____

_____

3. 나는 이 의견에 대해 부분적으로 동의한다. 다음의 몇 가지 이유 때문이다.

_____

_____

BODY 1

1. 일반적으로, 십대들은 학교에서 그들의 성적을 향상시키기 위해서 그들의 공부에 집중해야 한다.

_____

_____

2. 만약에 그들이 직업을 갖는다면 그들이 피곤해하거나 공부를 게을리하는 것은 당연하다.

_____

_____

3. 그들이 매일 피로에 지쳐서 집에 돌아올 경우 과제나 시험을 위한 복습을 더 이상 할 시간이 없을지도 모른다.

_____

_____

4. 이것에 덧붙여서, 십대들은 학교 활동에 참여하는 많은 기회를 가지고 있다.

_____

_____

5. 이것은 학교 밖에서 일하는 것보다 그들의 전반적인 성장을 더 발전시킬 수 있다.

_____

_____

6. 예를 들어, 그들이 캠핑 그리고 대회 같은 과외활동에 참가할 수 있다.

_____

_____

7. 그러한 것은 그들이 우정이나 협동심을 발전시키는 데 도움을 줄 수 있다.

_____

_____

8. 이러한 이유를 감안하면, 십대들이 그들의 학창시절 동안 직업을 구하는 게 아니고 그들의 학교 생활에 집중하는 것이 바람직하다.

_____

_____

BODY 2

1. 그러나 일하는 경험은 그들의 미래를 설계하는 데 훌륭한 기회이다.

_____

_____

2. 사실상, 일하는 학생들은 다양한 지식과 정보를 풍부한 경험으로부터 얻을 수 있고 심지어 직업적인 기술까지 연마할 수 있다.

_____

_____

3. 그들은 돈을 어떻게 관리하고 다양한 배경의 사람들과 어떻게 대화하는지를 배울 수 있다.

_____

_____

4. 그것은 또한 대학에서 전공을 결정하는 데 있어서 그리고 교육을 마친 이후에 그들이 추구하고자 하는 어떤 종류의 직업을 결정하는 때 그들에게 매우 도움이 될 수 있다.

_____

_____

5. 예를 들어, 몇몇의 학생들은 고등학교 때 레스토랑에서 보조로서 파트 타임 일을 했다.

_____

_____

6. 그 이후에 그들은 요리사가 되었다. 이처럼, 일 경험은 미래의 일을 결정하는 데 긍정적인 영향을 준다.

_____

_____

7. 덧붙여서, 학생들은 그들의 대학 수업료와 필요한 경비들을 위해 돈을 저축할 여력이 생긴다.

_____

_____

8. 이것은 어느 정도 그들의 부모님의 재정적인 부담이 줄어든다.

_____

_____

9. 이러한 이유들 때문에 학교에 다니는 동안 직업을 갖는 것은 학생들의 미래를 위해 보람 있는 경험이다.

_____

_____

CONCLUSION

1. 요약하면, 비록 몇 가지 단점들을 가지고 있지만, 학기 중에 일하는 것은, 십대들에게 상당히 도움이 된다.

_____

_____

2. 그것은 직업을 갖는다는 것은 학생들이 스스로 미래를 설계할 수 있고 그들의 대학 교육을 재정적으로 지원하는 것을 가능하게 만들기 때문이다.

_____

_____

3. 그러므로 부모들과 선생님들은 그들이 일을 못하게 할 것이 아니라, 그들을 지지해야 한다.

_____

_____

ANSWER

INTRODUCTION

1. It is a well-known fact that nowadays some workplaces employ teenagers who are still in school.

2. In this regard, some people argue that taking a job is a significant step for teens to gear up for their adulthood.

3. I partially agree with this comment. This following are some of the reasons.

BODY 1

1. In general, teens should focus on their studies to improve their grades in school.

2. It is natural for students to be tired and thus neglect their studies if they hold a job.

3. They may no longer have time to do their assignments or review for a test if they come home with exhaustion every day.

4. In addition to that, teenagers have many opportunities to attend school activities

5. , which could boost their overall growth rather than work outside of school.

6. They could, for instance, get involved in extracurricular activities, including camping or competitions

7. , which could help them develop friendship and cooperation.

8. Given these reasons, it makes sense for teenagers to concentrate on their school lives and not to find a job during their school years.

BODY 2

1. However, work experience is an excellent chance for teenage students to plan their future.

2. In fact, students working can acquire a far-reaching range of knowledge and information from a wealth of experience, even honing their professional skills.

3. They could learn how to manage money and communicate with people from various backgrounds.

4. It could also be a great help to them in making decisions about their majors in college and what kinds of job they would like to pursue after education.

5. Some students, for example, worked part-time at a restaurant as assistants when they were in high school.

6. Following that, they become chefs. Like this, work experience could have positive influences on the determination of a future job.

7. Additionally, students could afford to save money for their tuition fees and necessary expenses in college

8. , which somewhat curtails the financial burden on the parents.

9. For all these reasons, having a job while in school is a rewarding experience for the students' future.

CONCLUSION

1. To sum up, working during the academic year, although having a couple of drawbacks, is of great benefit to teenagers

2. , which is why having a job makes it possible for students to design the future on their own and support their university education financially.

3. Thus, parents and teachers should not deter them from working but support them.

PREVIOUS TEST

1. It is common practice for some students to take a gap year between high school and university in order to do charitable work abroad in underdeveloped countries. What are the advantages and disadvantages for younger people of doing volunteer work?

2. Some people think that people should choose their job based on income in order to provide security for their family.
Do you think money is an important factor when choosing a job?
What should other factors be considered?

3. Some people with a good education and experience in their field decide to move abroad to work. Why do you think that is?
What problems does this cause?

** 첨삭은 **ieltseasywriting.com**

5. Practical skill in University

> Many people believe that universities should offer theoretical knowledge rather than give vocational training to students. Do you agree or disagree?

ESSENTIAL VOCA

INTRODUCTION

교육의 질	the quality of education
이론적인 교육	theoretical education
전문적이고 수준 높은	specialized and sophisticated/professional and high-quality
실용적이고 기술적인 교육	practical and technical education
계속되어 온 문제	an ongoing(lasting) issue
~에 대한 논란	the controversy over/the debate over~
전보다	than ever before/than before/than in the past
이런 점에서	in this respect/in this light/in this regard
주장한다	argue/claim/state/believe/suggest/stress
이유들	reasons/causes/factors/culprits
~에 반대하다	be against(disagree with/be not in favor of)+Ⓝ
그 의견에 찬성하다	be for(be in favor of/agree with/support) the idea
자세히 설명하다	elaborate on/spell out/explain in full detail
다음과 같이	as follows

BODY 1(the importance of practical education)

학생들과 관련해서	concerning(regarding/as regards/with respect to) students
가장 효율적인 방법	the most effective way
직업교육	vocational(professional/occupational) education
~에 이점(우위)를 가지다	have an edge(advantage) in~
교육적인 도구/수단	an educational tool(measure/step/way)
앞으로/가까운 장래에	down the road/in the near(foreseeable) future
미래를 설계하다	design(project) the future
사회생활을 위한 준비를 하다	gear up for(prepare for/make preparation for) social life
직업전망	career prospects
특정한 자격을 갖추다	meet(hold/have/obtain) certain qualifications
기회를 얻다	obtain(gain/have) opportunities(chances/occasions)
고소득의 직업	well-paying jobs/high-paying jobs
직장을 구하다	land(obtain/have/gain) a job/look for employment/find employment
다양한 기술	various(diverse/a variety of) techniques(skills)
경험을 바탕으로/기본으로	based on experience
실질 훈련	on-the-job training
일과 관련된 배움	work-related learning
현장 체험 프로그램	hands-on programs
고용하다	employ/hire/engage/take on
믿을 수 있는	reliable/believable/credible/trustworthy
특별한 일을 어떻게 다루는지를 알다	know how to handle(deal with/cope with) specific tasks
더 유용한 정보를 발견하다	find out more useful information
생산성을 촉진하다	promote(generate/create/incur) productivity
인턴십	internship/a temporary position which students usually get work experience
기술 학교	technical school
이과 대학	a college of science
문과 대학	a liberal art college/a college of liberal arts

필수 과목들	required(compulsory/mandatory) subjects
선택 과목들	optional subjects
고등 교육	further(tertiary) education
학문적 수업에 주력하다	focus on(concentrate on/pay attention to) academic lectures(classes)
취업난	job crunch/job crisis/unemployment
높은 실업률	a high unemployment(jobless) rate/high unemployment
일을 시작하다	get down to work(task)/embark on working
문제없이/원활하게	without any hitches/without any troubles(problems/difficulties/concerns)
사회 생활에 익숙하다	be accustomed to(be used to/get used to) social life
새로운 환경에 적응하다	adjust(adapt) to a new environment
풍부한 경험	a wealth of(a great deal of/rich) experience

BODY 2(the importance of practical education)

회사들 측면에서 말하자면	when it comes to(in terms of/in the case of/in light of) companies
비용 절감	cost saving(cutting)
신입사원 교육으로부터 발생하는	resulting from(caused by/generated by) training recruits
지원자/구직자들	applicants/job seekers/job hunters
신입사원들	new employees/newcomers/new graduates/new workers
고용주와 사원	employers and employees(workers)
개인적이고 사회적인 낭비	personal and social waste
~에 유익하다	be of benefit to/be beneficial to~
대단한 도움이 되다	be a great help/be a good help
만약 ~이라면	provided(that) S+V
능력을 이용하다	exploit(harness/make use of/take advantage of) abilities
직업적인 기술을 발전시키다	develop(hone/advance) professional skills
힘든 상황	desperate(harsh/terrible) circumstances
변화의 요구에 보조를 맞추다	keep up with(catch up with) the changing demands

A는 책임이 있다	be down to A/A be responsible(accountable) for/A be to blame for
기술 향상을 초래하다	lead to(result in/give rise to/bring about) the development of skills
~하는 경향이 있다	be inclined to/tend to/be liable to/have a tendency to~
다시 말해서	in other words/to put it another way/that is/that is to say
의식을 높이다	raise(heighten/increase) awareness(consciousness)
교육제도를 개편하다	revamp(reshuffle/modify) education system
~에 긍정적인 영향을 끼치다	have a positive(affirmative/beneficial) impact(influence/effect) on~
~에 상당히 기여하다	make a considerable contribution to(contribute a great deal to)+Ⓝ

CONCLUSION

결론은	in conclusion/to conclude/to sum up
위에서 언급한 것처럼	as mentioned above/as stated above
모든 상황을 고려할 때	all things considered
~하고 생각하다/믿다	be of opinion that S+V
가치 있는 직업	a decent(desirable) job(occupation/profession)
비용을 줄이다	curtail(cut back on/cut down on/reduce/lessen) costs(expenses/expenditures/outlays)
설득력 있는	compelling/convincing/persuasive
직업교육에 관심을 갖다	pay attention to(take an interest in/get interested in) professional education
훨씬 더 ~할 것 같다	be far(much) more likely to~
~할 만한 가치가 있다	be worth(be worthy of)+Ⓝ

SENTENCE PRACTICE

INTRODUCTION

1. 사회가 발전함에 따라, 회사들은 전보다는 실용적인 기술을 가진 전문적이고 수준 높은 근로자들이 필요하다.

_____

_____

2. 이러한 점에서, 어떤 사람들은 대학들이 학생들에게 완전히 이론적인 지식을 교육시키는 대신에 실질적인 기술을 가르쳐야 한다고 주장한다.

_____

_____

3. 나는 동일한 생각을 가지고 있고 이유는 다음과 같다.

_____

_____

BODY 1

1. 학생들과 관련해서, 직업 교육을 받은 대학 졸업생들은 더 많은 직업 기회를 갖는 경향이 있다.

_____

_____

2. 다시 말해서, 그들은 다양한 기술을 요구하는 회사에서 특별한 일을 어떻게 다루는지를 알기 때문에 경쟁력에서 이점을 갖는다.

_____

_____

3. 많은 고용주들이 실용적인 기술들을 가진 지원자의 고용을 선호하는 것은 사실이다.

_____

_____

4. 이런 이유 때문에, 많은 학생들은 더 빨리 직업을 구하기 위해서 기술대학으로 바꾸고 있다.

_____

_____

5. 인문대학을 졸업한 졸업생들이 이공계 대학의 졸업생들보다 보수가 좋은 직업에 대한 낮은 가능성을 가지고 있다는 연구가 있다.

_____

_____

6. 인문대학은 주로 학문적 수업에 주력하기 때문이다.

_____

_____

7. 발전하는 기술과 함께, 이러한 상황은 더욱더 심화될 것이다.

_____

_____

8. 그러므로 대학이 학생들에게 실기교육을 제공하는 것은 더 나은 선택이다.

_____

_____

BODY 2

1. 회사들 측면에서 말하자면, 그들은 신입사원 교육으로부터 발생되는 시간과 경비를 절약할 수 있다.

_____

_____

2. 사실상, 회사는 신규 채용 후 직업훈련을 제공하고 있고, 이러한 것은 신입사원이나 고용주들에게 도움이 된다.

_____

_____

3. 그러나, 개인적이고 사회적인 낭비일 수 있다.

_____

_____

4. 만약 대학들이 직업훈련을 제공한다면, 회사의 비용이 줄어들 것이고, 근로자들은 학교에서 배운 기술을 가지고 그들의 일에서 능력을 활용하고 발전시킬 것이다.

_____

_____

5. 또한 이러한 것은 회사들이 힘든 상황에서 생존할 수 있게 하고 사업 분야에서 변화하는 요구에 따라갈 수 있게 할 것이다.

_____

_____

CONCLUSION

1. 결론은, 모든 상황을 고려할 때, 직업교육은 대학 졸업생들과 외사들에게 몇 가지 이점을 가지고 있다.

_____

_____

2. 왜냐하면, 그것은 학생들에게 미래에 가치 있는 직업을 갖게 하고 회사들은 비용을 절감할 수 있기 때문이다

_____

_____

3. 그러므로, 대학들과 관련된 사람들이 대학에서의 직업교육에 더 많은 관심을 갖는 것은 설득력이 있다.

_____

_____

ANSWER

INTRODUCTION

1. As society develops, companies need specialized and sophisticated employees with practical skills more than ever before.

2. In this respect, some people argue that universities should teach real skills to students instead of educating them with thoroughly theoretical knowledge.

3. I have the same idea, and the reasons are as follows.

BODY 1

1. Concerning students, university college graduates who have received vocational training tend to obtain more job opportunities.

2. In other words, they have an edge in competitiveness because they know how to handle specific tasks in companies that require various skills.

3. It is true that many employers prefer to hire applicants with practical skills.

4. For this reason, many students are shifting to technical colleges to land a job more quickly.

5. There is research that graduates from liberal arts colleges have a lower likelihood of a well-paid job than those from a college of science

6. , since liberal arts colleges mainly focus on academic lectures.

7. With developing technologies, this situation will be much more intensified.

8. Therefore, it is a better option for universities to offer practical training to students.

BODY 2

1. When it comes to companies, they can save time and cost resulting from training recruits.

2. In fact, they have provided vocational training after hiring new workers, which is of benefit to both new employees and employers.

3. However, it can be a personal and social waste.

4. Provided that universities offer professional training, companies' expenses will be reduced, and employees will exploit and develop their abilities in their businesses with skills gained in schools

5. , which would also enable companies to survive in harsh circumstances and keep up with the changing demands of the business area.

CONCLUSION

1. To conclude, all things considered, vocational education has several benefits for university graduates and companies

2. , since it allows students to have decent jobs in the future, and companies can curtail costs.

3. Hence, it is compelling for universities and people involved to pay more attention to professional education in universities.

PREVIOUS TEST

1. Some people say that in all levels of education, from primary schools to universities, too much time is spent on learning facts and not enough on learning practical skills.
Do you agree or disagree?

2. In some high schools, part of the curriculum requires students to participate in community work such as helping the elderly or disabled. In what way do children benefit from this?
Do you think it should be part of the curriculum?

3. In nearly all science courses at university, there are significantly more male students than female students.
What is the reason for this?
What could be done to balance out the numbers?

** 첨삭은 **ieltseasywriting.com**

Unit 3

Social issues

1. Overpopulation

2. Financial support

3. The crime rate

4. The death penalty

1. Overpopulation

> Overpopulation of urban areas has led to numerous problems. Identify serious ones and suggest ways that governments and individuals can tackle these problems.

ESSENTIAL VOCA

INTRODUCTION

과잉인구	overpopulation/excess(overflowing/surplus) population
계속 증가하는 인구	an ever-growing(ever-increasing/ever-rising) population
놀랍도록 증가해오고 있다	has(have) been alarmingly(amazingly/startlingly) on the rise(increase)
인구 집중	the concentration of population
주요도시들에 널리 퍼져 있다	be prevalent(general) in major cities
긴급한 문제	a pressing question/an urgent matter(problem)
근본적이고 중요한 원인들	underlying and vital(critical/crucial/significant) causes(reasons/culprits)
인구과잉에 의해 야기된	caused by(generated by/resulting from) overpopulation
심각한 결과들	serious results/grave consequences
정책/조치들	policies/initiatives
해법들과 함께	along with(coupled with/in company with) solutions
~에 대한 해결책으로써	as a solution to+Ⓝ
A를 고려하다	take A into account(consideration)/consider A
과잉인구에 대한 문제들을 제시하다	present(introduce/show) the problems of overpopulation

BODY 1(problems)

우선/먼저	first of all/above all/in the first place/first and foremost
몇 가지 주요한 문제들	a couple of(several/a few) main problems
발생하다/일어나다	come about/take place/break out/occur/generate
삶의 질을 악화시키다	deteriorate(aggravate/compromise) the quality of living(life)
전반적으로	overall/in general/generally
한 예로써	for one thing/for instance/for example/to illustrate
기여 요인	a contributory(contributing) factor
열악한 위생	poor sanitation(hygiene)
인구과잉의 환경적 피해	the environmental damage(impact) of overpopulation
이산화탄소로 인한 공기 오염	air pollution resulting from carbon dioxide emission
중대한 건강문제	a significant(serious) health problem(concern/trouble)
질병을 초래하다	bring about(lead to/result in/give rise to) illness(disease/sickness)
과밀/혼잡 도시	an overpopulated(overcrowded/bustling) city
교통 혼잡	traffic congestion(jam)
주택 부족 문제	the housing shortage problem
열악한 경제상황	poor(atrocious/deteriorating) economic situations(circumstances/surroundings)
무거운 재정적 부담	a heavy financial strain(burden/pressure)
재정적 어려움을 겪다	undergo(suffer from/go through/experience) financial difficulties(troubles/concerns)
~에게 위협을 가하다	threaten(pose a threat to/present a serious threat to)+Ⓝ
위험한 상황에 빠지다	fall into risky(dangerous/precarious) circumstances/be at stake/be at risk
문제에 직면하다	face(confront/encounter) problems(difficulties/concerns/challenges)
실업증가	the rise of unemployment(jobless)
실업으로부터 야기된 가난으로부터 벗어나다	escape from poverty caused(generated) by unemployment
높은(낮은) 범죄율	the(a) high(low) crime rate
부자들	the haves/the rich/the wealthy/the affluent/the privileged
가난한 사람들	the have-nots/the needy/those in need/the poor/the unprivileged
부자들과 가난한 사람들의 격차	the gap(gulf) between the haves and the have-nots

가난에 시달리는 나라들	poverty-stricken nations/impoverished countries/poverty nations
소외계층	the disadvantaged/the minority/the underprivileged
이와 같이	like this/with this/in this manner/in this regard
~에게 악영향을 끼치다	have(exert) adverse(detrimental/harmful) influences(effects/impacts) on~

BODY 2(solutions)

해법에 대해 말하자면	when it comes to(in light of/with respect to) solutions
해결하다	settle/tackle/address/solve/resolve/sort out/unravel
가능한 조치를 취하다	take feasible(possible/workable/viable/practicable) actions(steps/measures)
도시 지역들	urban(city) areas/metro regions
특히	in particular/particularly/specially/especially
거주 지역을 확장하다	expand(enlarge/widen) residential districts(areas)
~의 근교에	on the outskirts on~/in the suburbs of~
인구의 분산	population decentralization
인구를 분산시키다	disperse(decentralize) population
인구 집중을 완화시키다	lessen(alleviate/relieve/ease) the concentration of population
잘 정비된 교통 시스템	a well-organized(well-maintained) transportation system
대중교통	public transportation/public transport
강화하다	beef up/reinforce/strengthen/fortify/intensity
사회 구조	the social fabric(system)
사회기반 시설을 개선하다	Improve(develop) social infrastructure
사회복지 시설	social welfare(service) facilities
지역 사회의 산업을 촉진하다	boost(develop/accelerate/fuel/facilitate) industries in local areas
균형 있게 성장하다	develop(flourish/prosper) in a balanced way(manner)
재정적 지원	financial grants(aid/support/assistance)/funding assistance
A에게 B를 제공하다	provide(furnish/supply) A with B/provide(furnish/supply) B to(for) A
~할 여력이 있다(시간/돈)	can afford to/be capable of~

범죄율을 줄이다	cut down on(cut back on/reduce/alleviate) the crime rate
범죄를 억제하다	curb(restraint/retard/inhibit) crimes
가장 중요한 것은	most importantly/first and most importantly
더욱이	moreover/furthermore/in addition/what is more
A뿐만 아니라 B도	B as well as A/A not only but also B
이외에도	besides/aside from/other than
어느 정도	to some degree(extent)/somewhat/more or less
A와 B를 구별하다	tell(distinguish/differentiate) A from B
~하지 않는 경향이 있다	have no tendency to/do not tend to~
다시 말해서	that is to say/that is/in other words/to put it another way
이것을 위해서	to this end/to that end
이러한 맥락에서/따라서	in this context/therefore/thus/as a result/consequently/hence

CONCLUSION

결론적으로/요약하면	in conclusion/to conclude/to sum up
고려해 볼 때/가정한다면	given that S+V/given ⓝ
긴 안목에서/결국에는	in the long run/after all/in the end
~을 분명히 하다	shed light on~
분명하다	it is clear-cut(certain/apparent/clear) that S+V
정책을 세우다	set(set up/establish/formulate/shape) a policy
광범위한	far-reaching(far-flung/extensive)
A를 실행하다	practice(enforce/implement/carry out) A/put A in practice(force)
책임을 공유하다	share responsibility
~에 책임이 있다	take(have) responsibility for/be responsible(accountable) for~
이치에 맞다	make sense/stand to reason/be logical

SENTENCE PRACTICE

INTRODUCTION

1. 세계의 대부분 지역에서, 인구는 놀랍도록 증가하고 있고 주로 주요 도시에 널리 퍼져 있다.

_____

_____

2. 그리고 그것은 세계의 가장 큰 걱정 중의 하나가 되고 있다.

_____

_____

3. 국민들과 정부들은 심각하게 이 문제를 고려해야만 한다.

_____

_____

4. 이 에세이는 과잉 인구에 대한 해법들과 함께 문제들을 제시할 것이다.

_____

_____

BODY 1

1. 몇 가지 문제들이 인구 과잉 때문에 발생한다.

_____

_____

2. 우선, 인구 과잉은 많은 도시에서 삶의 질을 악화시킨다.

_____

_____

3. 한 예로서, 인구 과밀과 열악한 위생시설을 갖춘 주거는 중대한 건강 문제들을 만들어 내고 질병들을 일으킬 수 있다.

_____

_____

4. 계속되는 인구 증가의 다른 심각한 결과는 실업의 증가이다.

_____

_____

5. 이것은 범죄율 증가를 초래한다. 왜냐하면, 일부 사람들은 실업에 의해 발생된 가난으로부터 벗어나기 위해서 범죄를 택하기 때문이다.

_____

_____

6. 마지막으로, 과잉 인구에 의해서 일어난 환경적인 피해가 심각하다.

_____

_____

7. 그것은 큰 도시들에서의 급격한 차량의 증가는 교통문제뿐만 아니라 이산화탄소로 인한 공기 오염을 발생시키기 때문이다.

_____

_____

8. 이와 같이, 도시인구의 과도한 증가는 몇 가지 부정적인 측면을 가지고 있다.

_____

_____

BODY 2

1. 해법에 대해 말하자면, 사람들과 정부들은 대도시에서의 인구 과잉을 해결하기 위한 실행 가능한 조치를 해야 한다.

_____

_____

2. 정부는 대도시에 주택 문제를 해결해야 한다.

_____

_____

3. 특히 도시 인구의 분산을 위해서 주요 도시 외곽에 거주 지역을 확장해서 주택 문제를 해결해야 한다.

_____

_____

4. 실업 문제에 대해서는, 정부는 인구를 분산하기 위해서 특히 지역 사회에 산업을 촉진하고 고용을 증진시켜야 한다.

_____

_____

5. 이러한 것은 실업과 대도시에서의 범죄율을 또한 낮출 수 있다.

_____

_____

6. 마지막으로, 인구 과잉에 의한 환경문제와 관련해서, 시민들은 그들의 차보다 버스나 지하철 같은 대중교통을 이용해야만 한다.

_____

_____

7. 이를 위해서, 시민들이 그들을 편리하게 이용할 수 있도록 잘 정비된 대중교통 시스템을 만들어야 한다.

_____

_____

8. 서울을 예로 들면, 교통혼잡과 서울에서의 인구집중을 완화시키기 위해서 교통 시스템이 잘 정비되어 오고 있다.

_____

_____

9. 그 결과, 어느 정도 교통 문제뿐만 아니라 대기오염 문제도 해결하는 데 도움이 되고 있다.

_____

_____

CONCLUSION

1. 결론적으로, 도시에서의 인구 과잉에 의해 야기된 문제들이 광범위한 것은 분명하다.

_____

_____

2. 만약 사람들과 정부가 위에서 언급한 방법으로 책임을 공유한다면, 그들은 과잉 인구 문제들을 해결할 것이다.

_____

_____

ANSWER

INTRODUCTION

1. In most parts of the world, the population has been alarmingly on the rise and mainly prevalent in major cities

2. , and it has become one of the world's biggest concerns.

3. Individuals and governments have to take this issue into account seriously.

4. This essay will present the problems of overpopulation along with solutions.

BODY 1

1. A couple of main problems come about because of overpopulation.

2. First of all, overpopulation deteriorates the quality of living in many cities.

3. For one thing, overcrowding and housing with poor sanitation cause significant health problems, bringing about illnesses.

4. Another serious result of an ever-growing population is the rise of unemployment

5. , which could lead to an increasing crime rate because some choose crimes to escape from poverty caused by unemployment.

6. Lastly, the environmental damage generated by overpopulation is considerable.

7. It is because the rapid increase in vehicles in large cities gives rise to air pollution resulting from carbon dioxide emission as well as traffic problems.

8. Like this, the excessive growth of urban population has some adverse aspects.

BODY 2

1. When it comes to solutions, individuals and governments should take feasible steps to settle excess population in big cities.

2. Governments should sort out the housing problem.

3. In particular, they ought to expand the residential districts for population decentralization on the outskirts of the main urban cities.

4. In light of the unemployment problem, governments should boost industries and promote employment, especially in local areas to disperse population

5. , which can lower unemployment and the crime rate in the major cities as well.

6. Finally, as regards environmental concerns from overpopulation, citizens had better use public transport like buses and underground rather than their cars.

7. To this end, governments are supposed to build a well-organized transportation system for citizens to use them conveniently.

8. Take Seoul, for example, where the traffic system has been well-maintained to lessen the concentration of population and the traffic congestion.

9. As a result, its policy is of help to solve not only air pollution but also traffic problems to some extent.

CONCLUSION

1. In conclusion, it is clear-cut that the problems caused by overpopulation in urban areas are far-reaching.

2. If individuals and governments share responsibility in the way mentioned above, they will resolve the difficulties of overpopulation.

PREVIOUS TEST

1. Nowadays, people living in large cities face many problems in their daily lives. What are these problems? Do you think the government should encourage people to move to smaller towns? (2018.)

2. With increasing populations and ever-growing urban centers, many countries are losing their natural beauty spots. What benefits are there to protect places of natural beauty? How can this be solved?

3. The population of most cities is growing as people move to cities to find work and new opportunities.
What problems does overpopulation in cities cause?
How can these problems be solved?

** 첨삭은 **ieltseasywriting.com**

2. Financial support

Many advanced countries are giving financial aid to underdeveloped countries. However, this has not solved the problem of poverty in these nations, and so other types of help should be provided. To what extent do you agree or disagree with this statement?

ESSENTIAL VOCA

INTRODUCTION

선진국들	advanced(developed) countries
후진국들	underdeveloped(undeveloped/lower-developed/backward) countries
열악한 경제상황	poor(atrocious/deteriorating) economic situations(circumstances/surroundings)
국제적인 차원에서	on a global(international) scale(level)
재정적 지원	financial(economic/monetary) assistance(support/aid/help/fund)
논쟁의 문제	a controversial issue/a matter of argument
실행 가능한 해결책	a feasible(workable/viable/practicable/reasonable) solution
관련된 해결책들	a relevant(related/associated/involved) solution
접근법들/방법들	approaches/procedures/ways/methods/manners/measures
도움이 되다	be of help/be helpful
해결하다	settle/tackle/address/solve/sort out/unravel
개선하다	improve/better/make better
내 의견으로는	in my opinion/from my point of view/in my judgment
주장하다	argue/claim/assert/believe/maintain

BODY 1(disagree)

확실히	certainly/strongly/firmly/definitely/obviously
재정적 도움을 주다	give(offer/provide) financial help(grants/support)
도움이 절실히 필요한 사람에게 도달하지 않는다	do not reach the people who desperately need assistance
주요한 원인	the underlying(principal/main/major/primary) cause
사회적 요인들	social factors(reasons/causes/sources)
고질적인 문제들	chronic problems(issues/concerns/troubles/difficulties)
비효율성과 부정적인 결과들	ineffectiveness and unfavorable consequences
기여 요인	a contributory(contributing) factor
~에 의해 야기된	resulting from/caused by/generated by/originated by
정치적 기득권층(지배층)	the political establishment
부자들	the haves/the rich/the wealthy/the affluent/the privileged
가난한 사람들	the have-nots/the needy/those in need/the poor/the unprivileged
부자들과 가난한 사람들의 격차	the gap(gulf) between the haves and the have-nots
가난에 시달리는	poverty-stricken nations/impoverished countries/poverty nations
최하층/상류층	the underclass/the upper class
취약한 사람들	the vulnerable/vulnerable people
소외계층	the underprivileged/the disadvantaged/the minority/the unfortunate
약자들	the underdog/the weaker
적절한 교육의 부족	a lack of proper education
사회적 불공정(불평등)과 교육의 기회 부족	social injustice and lack of opportunity in education
있는 그대로	as it is/as it comes
상대적 박탈감을 느끼다	feel a sense of relative deprivation
삶의 질을 악화시키다	deteriorate(aggravate/compromise) the quality of living
~하는 경향이 있다	tend to/have a tendency to/be inclined to/be liable to~
발전할 기회를 잃어버리다	lose opportunities(chances)to advance
실업증가	the rise of unemployment(jobless)
심하고 긴 고통	intense and prolonged pain(distress/suffering)

기관들/단체들	organizations/institutions/agencies
정치적 부패	political corruption(decay)
권력을 이용하다	use(take advantages of/make use of/employ/exploit) power
도덕성/윤리성	morality/ethicality
정치적 부패와 관련되다	be related to(be involved with/be associated with) political corruption
일반적 관행으로 여겨지다	be regarded as(be considered as) a standard practice
A를 당연한 것으로 생각하다	take A for granted
경제적 어려움에 처해 있다	be in economic(financial) troubles/have economic(financial) difficulties
극심한 재정적 어려움	extreme(heavy) financial hardships(difficulties/troubles/concerns)
재정적 부담	a financial strain(burden/pressure)
외부의 지원에 의지하다	resort to(make resort to/depend on/rely on) outside help
A가 책임이 있다	A take(have) responsibility for/A be responsible(accountable) for/A be to blame for
다시 말해서	that is to say/that is/in other words/to put it another way
예를 들어	to illustrate/for instance/for example/for one thing
그것을(이것을) 위해서	to that(this) end
마찬가지로/또한	as well/also/likewise/too
~에 따르면	according to~
이러한 맥락에서/따라서	in this context/therefore/thus/as a result/consequently/hence

BODY 2(other approaches)

다른 한편으로는	meanwhile/on the other hand/on the flip side
가장 중요한 것은	most importantly/first and most importantly
교육적인 접근	educational access(approach/means)
재정적 도움 대신에	in place of(in lieu of/instead of) financial support
A에게 B를 제공하다	provide(furnish/support) A with B/provide(furnish/support) B to(for) A
농업기술들	agricultural skills
학교 시설	school facilities

다양한 교육 자료들	a broad(wide/great) range of educational materials(references/resources)
시민들을 그들의 권리를 알게 하다	enable(allow) citizens to be aware of their right
~에 상당히 기여하다	contribute considerably(a great deal) to(make a considerable contribution to)+Ⓝ
가난으로부터 벗어나다	get out of(lift out of/escape from) poverty/put an end to poverty
실질적인 영향을 끼치다	have substantial(practical/actual/real) effects(impacts/influences) on
대단히 노력하다	make(exert) great(considerable) efforts
부패를 억제하다	curb(restraint/retard/inhibit/deter) corruption
부패에 맞서 싸우다	fight against corruption
다루다/해결하다	cope with/deal with/handle
책임을 공유하다	share responsibility
(A와 B) 사이에 공백을 메우다	bridge the gap(gulf) between A and B
~때문에	due to(because of/owing to/on account of)+Ⓝ
긴 안목에서/결국에는	in the long run/after all/in the end
A를 실행하다	carry out(practice/implement) A/put A into practice/put A into action
야기하다/초래하다	lead to(give rise to/result in/bring about)+Ⓝ
균형 있게 발전하다	develop(improve/flourish) in a balanced way
이와 같이/이렇게 하여	like this/in this way/in this manner/in this regard

CONCLUSION

결론적으로/요약하면	in conclusion/to conclude/to sum up
~에 찬성하다	agree with/be in favor of/be for/approve of~
고려해 볼 때/가정한다면	given that S+V/given+Ⓝ
힘든 조치들	demanding(daunting/challenging/tough) measures(approaches/initiatives/policies)
이 복잡한 문제를 마무리 짓다	put up end to this complicated problem
전통적인 속담을 사용하자면	to use a traditional proverb
해법들과 함께	along with(coupled with/in company with) solutions

SENTENCE PRACTICE

INTRODUCTION

1. 선진국들이 저개발국들에게 경제적 원조를 해야만 하는지에 대한 주제는 논쟁의 문제가 되고 있다.

_____

_____

2. 어떤 사람들은 재정적인 지원은 후진국의 빈곤 해결에 도움이 된다고 주장한다.

_____

_____

3. 내 의견으로는, 그러나, 재정적 도움은 그들 나라의 상황을 개선시키지 않고 다른 접근법이 실행되어야 한다.

_____

_____

BODY 1

1. 나는 경제적 지원은 후진국의 열악한 경제 상황을 개선시키지 않는다고 확실히 믿는다.

_____

_____

2. 첫 번째 이유는 사회 전반에 걸친 부패가 가난한 나라가 직면한 고질적인 문제들 중 하나이기 때문이다.

_____

_____

3. 비록 선진국이 재정적인 도움을 준다 해도, 그것은 절실하게 도움이 필요한 일반 사람에게는 도달하지 않는다.

_____

_____

4. 이것은 정치가들과 영향력 있는 사업가들과 같은 기득권층이 대부분의 금전상의 원조를 가져가기 때문이다.

_____

_____

5. 그것은 부자와 가난한 사람들의 격차를 더 크게 만들고 또한 사회적 문제들을 일으킨다.

_____

_____

6. 다른 문제는 가난한 나라에서의 교육의 부족이다.

_____

_____

7. 교육의 부족은 국민들이 그들의 권리를 알지 못하는 경향이 있고 가난을 있는 그대로 받아들인다.

_____

_____

8. 이것은 개개인 그리고 국가가 발전할 기회를 잃어버리는 것이다.

_____

_____

9. 이러한 이유 때문에, 그들은 부자나라들로부터 받은 경제적 도움에도 불구하고 가난에서 벗어날 수가 없다.

_____

_____

BODY 2

1. 한편으로는, 경제적인 지원 대신에 가난한 나라들을 돕기 위한 다른 조치가 있어야만 한다.

_____

_____

2. 가장 중요한 것은, 후진국들은 질 좋은 교육 체계, 시설들 그리고 자료들과 같은 교육적 지원을 경제적 정치적 개선을 위해 받는 것이 필요하다.

_____

_____

3. 교육을 가난한 나라의 시민들이 그들의 권리뿐만 아니라 기술과 재능을 가진 인간으로서 자기의 잠재력을 알게 할 수 있다.

_____

_____

4. 이러한 것은 더 나아가 경제적인 발전과 부패 단절과 같은 정치적 개혁에 상당히 기여한다.

_____

_____

5. 사실상, 요즘 많은 선진국들과 월드 비전(WORLD VISION) 같은 국제기구들은 경제적 어려움에 처해 있는 국가들을 위해 교육적인 지원을 하고 있다.

_____

_____

6. 예를 들어, 그들은 실질적인 농업기술을 가르치고 학교를 건립하며 다양한 교육 자료들을 제공한다.

_____

_____

7. 조사에 따르면, 이 정책은 빈곤국가에서의 사람들의 삶에 실질적인 영향을 주고 있다.

_____

_____

8. 이러한 맥락에서, 교육적인 접근은 빈곤에서 벗어나기 위한 긴 안목으로 보면 정치적 부정부패에 맞서기 위한 최상의 해법이다.

_____

_____

CONCLUSION

1. 결론은, 나는 경제적 지원이 후진국의 가난을 해결하지 못해 오고 있다는 의견에 전적으로 동의한다.

_____

_____

2. 비록 이 복잡한 문제를 마무리 짓는 것은 힘든 일이지만, 자금 지원 대신에, 교육적인 지원이 빈곤국가들에게 실질적인 도움을 줄 수 있다.

_____

_____

3. 전통적인 속담을 사용하자면, 경제적으로 후진국들은, 단지 고기를 받는 것보다 고기 잡는 방법을 배우는 것이 더 낫기 때문이다.

_____

_____

ANSWER

INTRODUCTION

1. The topic of whether developed countries should give financial assistance to undeveloped nations has become a controversial issue.

2. Some people argue that financial support to underdeveloped countries is of great help to address the problem of poverty.

3. In my opinion, though, funding does not improve the situations in those countries, and another approach should be carried out.

BODY 1

1. I certainly believe that financial help does not improve the poor economic situation in underdeveloped countries.

2. The first reason is that corruption across all society is one of the chronic problems low developed countries face.

3. Even though wealthy nations give financial help, it does not reach the people who desperately need assistance.

4. It is because the establishment such as politicians and influential people in business take most of the financial grants.

5. It leads to an even greater gulf between the haves and the have-nots, giving rise to social problems as well.

6. Another issue is the lack of education in poverty-stricken countries.

7. They have no tendency to be aware of their rights and accept their poverty as it is

8. , which loses their opportunities for individuals and nations to advance.

9. For these reasons, they could not get out of poverty despite the economic aid they receive from wealthier nations.

BODY 2

1. Meanwhile, in place of financial support, there should be other measures to help undeveloped countries.

2. Most importantly, it is necessary for underdeveloped countries to receive educational support, for economic and political improvement, including a good quality school system, facilities, and materials.

3. Education enables citizens in undeveloped countries to be aware, not just of their rights, but also of their potential as human beings with skills and talents

4. , which can further contribute significantly to the economic development and political reform like curbing corruption.

5. In fact, nowadays many advanced countries and organizations involved like World Vision provide educational support for countries that are in economic trouble.

6. To illustrate, they teach practical agricultural skills, build schools, and offer a broad range of teaching materials.

7. According to research, this policy has substantial influences on people's lives in impoverished countries.

8. In this context, the educational access could be far and away the best solution to lift out of poverty and fight against corruption in the long run.

CONCLUSION

1. To conclude, I completely agree with the view that financial support has not solved the poverty of underdeveloped nations.

2. Though putting an end to this complicated problem is demanding, instead of funding assistance, an educational fund could be of real help to poverty nations

3. , since it is better for backward countries financially, to use a traditional proverb, to learn how to fish rather than only receive fish.

PREVIOUS TEST

1. More developing countries are given aid from international organizations to help them in their development plans. Some people argue that financial aid is important, but others suggest that practical aid and advice are more important. Discuss both views and give your opinion.

2. Improvements in health, education, and trade are essential for the development of poorer nations. However, the governments of richer nations should take more responsibility for helping the poorer nations in such areas. To what extent do you agree or disagree?

3. Many people think that countries have a moral obligation to help each other, while others argue that the aid money is misspent by the government that receives it, so international aid should not be given to the poor countries in the world anymore. Discuss the two views of international aid, and give your opinion.

** 첨삭은 **ieltseasywriting**.com

3. The crime rate

The crime rate has increased rapidly around the world. Discuss some causes for this rise and suggest workable solutions to this problem.

ESSENTIAL VOCA

INTRODUCTION

범죄율	the crime rate
계속 증가하는 범죄율	the ever-increasing(ever-rising/ever-growing) crime rate
상당히	significantly/considerably/dramatically/rapidly/fairly
범죄율이 증가해 오고 있다	the crime rate has been on the rise(increase)
~라는 것은 사실이다	it is a fact that S+V
범죄자들	criminals/offenders/culprits
청소년 범죄	youth crime/juvenile delinquency
범죄를 저지르다	commit(carry out) a crime(sin)
근본적인 원인들	underlying(fundamental) causes(culprits/grounds/reasons)
접근법/방법들	approaches/methods/ways/techniques
관련된 기관	relevant organizations/organization involved
~에 대한 해결책으로써	as a solution to+Ⓝ
범죄율을 줄이다	cut back on(cut down on/reduce/lessen/curtail) the crime rate
해결하다/다루다	tackle/address/deal with/cope with/sort out/settle/resolve
실행 가능한 해결책을 생각해 내다	come up with(figure out) a feasible(workable/viable) solution
자세히 설명하다	spell out/elaborate on/explain in full detail

BODY 1(causes)

우선	to begin with/first of all/first and foremost
몇 가지 문제들	a couple of(a few/several) issues
물질주의	materialism
가난에서 벗어나기 위해서	in order to(so as to) lift(emerge/get out of) poverty
압도적인/극심한/과도한	overwhelming/extreme/severe
재정적 어려움을 겪다	undergo(suffer from/go through/experience) financial difficulties
경제적 어려움에 처해 있다	be in economic troubles
경제적인 상태가 좋지 않다	be in unfavorable(terrible) economic condition
가난한 사람들	the have-nots/impoverished people/the needy/those in need/the poor/the unprivileged
소외계층	the disadvantaged/the minority/the underprivileged
취약한 사람들	the vulnerable/vulnerable people
기득권층	the establishment
부자들	the haves/the rich/the wealthy/the affluent/the privileged
부자들과 가난한 사람들의 격차	the gap(gulf) between the haves and the have-nots
강도를 저지르다	commit(carry out) a robbery
A에게서 B를 빼앗다	rob(deprive) A of B
전반적으로	overall/in general/generally
(사건 등이) 발생하다	break out/arise/take place/happen/occur
폭력적이고 선정적인 내용	violent and sexual(suggestive) contents
도덕성 결여	a lack(deficient) of morality
적절한 교육의 부족	a lack of proper education
실업증가	the rise of unemployment(jobless)
사회로부터 소외되다	be isolated from(be far from/be excluded from) society
범죄에 의존하다	resort to(have resort to/rely on/depend on) a crime
폭음	binge drink/heavy(excessive) drinking
약물 남용	drug abuse/overdose/substance abuse
마약 밀매	drug trafficking(traffic/smuggling)

마약과 알코올의 위험성	the dangers of drug and alcohol
중독자	an addict(-holic)
중독성이 있는	addictive
~에 중독되다	be addicted to/get addicted to/get obsessed with/be poisoned by
통제력을 잃다	lose control/lose one's grip
범죄에 대해 둔감해지다	get insensitive about(be indifferent to) a crime
법을 회피하다	skirt around the rules/evade(avoid/shun) the laws
공격자/가해자	an attacker/an assailant/an aggressor
일반 대중	the public/the general public/citizens
불우한 어린 시절	a deprived(underprivileged/disadvantaged) childhood
불우한 가정환경	a poor family background/the poor home environment
맞벌이 가정	a double-income family/a dual-income family
청소년 비행문제	the problem of delinquency
자살하다	commit suicide/kill oneself/take one's own life/suicide
모방범죄를 저지르다	commit a copy crime(offense)
젊은이들에게 악영향을 끼치다	have(exert) adverse(detrimental/harmful) influences(effects) on the youth
~에 해가 되다	be harmful to(be pernicious to/be injurious to)+Ⓝ
결과적으로/따라서	consequently/as a result/therefore/hence/thus/in this context

BODY 2(solutions)

다른 한편으로는	on the flip side/on the contrary/on the other hand
가장 중요한 것은	most importantly/first and most importantly
부자들과 가난한 사람들의 빈부격차를 메우다	bridge the gap(gulf) between the affluent and the needy
사회 복지	social welfare(service)
교육적인 접근	educational access(approach/method/way)
사회적 지위	social status(position/standing)
그것에 덧붙여서	in addition to that/on top of that/not only that

기관들/단체들	organizations/institutions/agencies
사법 제도	a justice(legal) system
강화된 법	an enhanced(strengthened/intensified) law
법을 제정하다	legislate(make/enact/create) a law
시행하다	implement/practice/carry out/enforce
강화하다	beef up/reinforce/strengthen/fortify/intensity
정책을 세우다	set(set up/establish/formulate/shape) a policy
강력한 법적 조치를 취하다	take a strong legal measure(step/action)
감시카메라	security cameras/surveillance cameras
벌금과 처벌의 강력한 시스템	a stricter system of penalties and punishments
수사 기술	investigation(detective) techniques(skills)
법을 준수하다	comply with(abide by/observe/keep/obey) the law
~에 대한 혐의로	on suspicion of~
법을 어기다	violate(break/infringe) the law/be against the law
엄중 단속하다	crack down on/clamp down on/control strongly
처벌하다	penalize/carry out a punishment/punish
형사처벌	criminal punishment(persecution)
과한 처벌	severe(heavy/intensive) punishment
최고 형량	a maximum punishment(penalty)
사형	capital punishment/death penalty/execution/the punishment of death
종신형	life imprisonment/life in prison/life sentence/imprisonment in life
범죄자에게 종신형을 선고하다	sentence offenders to life in prison
A에게 B를 제공하다	provide(supply/furnish) A with B/provide(supply/furnish) B to(for) A
출소 후	after release(discharge) from prison
억제책으로서	as a deterrent
재정적 지원	financial(economic/monetary) aid(assistance)
치료 프로그램	intervention programs
갱생(재생)프로그램	rehabilitation systems

죄를 반성하다	reflect on wrongdoing
범죄자들을 갱생시키다	rehabilitate criminals
적응하다	adjust to(adapt) to/get adjusted to+Ⓝ
지역 봉사 활동	community services/community programs
시설들	facilities/equipment
범죄를 근절하다	stamp out(root out/eradicate/uproot) crimes
이것을(그것을) 위해서	to this end/to that end
다시 말해서	that is to say/that is/in other words/to put it another way
긴 안목에서/결국에는	in the long run/after all/in the end

CONCLUSION

결론적으로/요약하면	in conclusion/to conclude/to sum up
위에서 언급한 것처럼	as stated(mentioned) above
분석하다	analyze/research/examine
이러한 방법으로	in this way/in this regard/in this respect
이치에 맞다	make sense/stand to reason/be logical
책임을 공유하다	share responsibility(accountability/liability)
범죄 없는 사회	a crime-free society

SENTENCE PRACTICE

INTRODUCTION

1. 범죄율이 세계적으로 상당히 증가해 오고 있다는 것은 사실이다.

_____

_____

2. 비록 정부와 관련기관들은 적극적으로 이 문제를 해결하려고 적극적으로 노력해 오고 있지만,

_____

_____

3. 범죄율을 줄이는 것은 쉽지 않다.

_____

_____

4. 이 에세이에서, 나는 증가하는 범죄율의 몇 가지 원인들과 실행 가능한 해결책을 자세히 설명하겠다.

_____

_____

Unit

3

Social issues

BODY 1

1. 우선, 범죄가 증가하고 있는 데는 몇 가지 이유가 있다.

_____

_____

2. 첫 번째, 부자들과 가난한 사람들의 빈부격차는 상당히 심화되고 있다.

_____

_____

3. 일반적으로, 어려움을 겪는 일부의 빈곤한 사람들은 삶의 어려움에 대한 해결책으로서 범죄를 저지르는 경향이 있다.

_____

_____

4. 더욱이, 그들은 그들이 당국으로부터 적절한 대우를 받지 못한다고 믿고 사회로부터 소외된다고 느끼는 경향이 있다.

_____

_____

5. 이런 상황에서, 소외 계층이 그들 자신의 필요를 충족하기 위해서 위법 행위에 의지한다.

_____

_____

6. 예를 들면, 그들은 생존을 위한 현금이나 물건을 얻기 위해 강도를 저지른다.

_____

_____

7. 두 번째는, 도덕성이 최근에 현저히 약해지고 있고 물질주의는 오늘날 과거보다 더욱 강해지고 있다.

_____

_____

8. 다시 말해서, 사람에 대한 가치를 그들의 인격과 도덕성보다 물질적인 부에 두고 있다.

_____

_____

9. 이러한 가치관에 대한 변화는 사람들에게 범죄를 저지르도록 유도한다.

_____

_____

BODY 2

1. 결과적으로, 정부는 이 문제를 해결하기 위해서 노력하는 것이 중요하다.

_____

_____

2. 우선, 그들은 부자들과 가난한 사람들의 빈부격차를 줄여야 한다.

_____

_____

3. 그들이 이것을 성취하기 위해 사회적 복지와 교육 시스템이 효율적으로 계획되어야 한다.

_____

_____

4. 이러한 것들은, 낮은 사회적 위치에 있는 사람들에게 나은 미래를 찾을 수 있도록 동등하게 기회들을 제공해야
한다.

_____

_____

5. 그것에 덧붙여서, 범죄율이 더 증가하는 것을 막기 위해 사법제도가 강화되어야 한다.

_____

_____

6. 다시 말해서, 강력한 법 집행과 형사처벌이 필요하다.

_____

_____

7. 그것을 위해서 정부는 경찰들에게 최신 장비와 발전된 수사 기술을 제공해야 한다.

_____

_____

8. 이뿐만 아니라, 범죄자들이 출소 후 사회에 적응할 수 있도록 적절한 갱생 프로그램이 시행되어야 한다.

_____

_____

CONCLUSION

1. 결론은 위에서 언급한 것처럼, 범죄 증가의 몇 가지 이유들이 있고, 그것을 해결하는 접근법들 또한 제시되었다.

_____

_____

2. 범죄들에 대한 이유들을 철저하게 분석함으로써, 문제를 해결하기 위해 적절한 해결책들이 적용되어야만 한다.

_____

_____

3. 이러한 방법으로, 사회는 범죄 없는 사회가 될 수 있다.

_____

_____

ANSWER

INTRODUCTION

1. It is a fact that the crime rate has been on the rise significantly in various parts of the world.

2. Even though governments and relevant organizations have been actively trying to address the issue.

3. It is not easy to cut down on the crime rate.

4. In this essay, I will spell out several culprits and feasible solutions to the increasing crime rate.

BODY 1

1. To begin with, there are a couple of issues that cause the crime rate to rise.

2. First, the gap between the haves and the have-nots has considerably widened.

3. In general, some impoverished people who have undergone financial difficulties tend to commit crimes as a solution to life's hardship.

4. Moreover, they usually believe they do not obtain proper treatment from the authorities and have a tendency to feel isolated from society.

5. In these circumstances, the disadvantaged resort to misconduct to meet their own needs.

6. For instance, they commit a robbery to acquire just money or other items for survival.

7. Second, morality has noticeably weakened in recent years, and materialism has become much stronger today than it was in the past.

8. That is to say, a person's worth puts in his/her material wealth rather than in their character and morality.

9. These changes in values have led people to commit a crime.

BODY 2

1. Consequently, it is vital for governments to make considerable efforts to tackle the issue.

2. Firstly, they should bridge the gulf between the affluent and the needy.

3. For them to achieve it, social welfare and education systems should be planned efficiently

4. , which should provide opportunities equally for people in low social statuses to find a better future.

5. In addition to that, justice systems should be reinforced to deter the crime rate from a further increase.

6. In other words, the strict implementation of laws and criminal punishments are necessary.

7. To that end, governments should furnish police officers with the latest equipment and advanced investigation techniques.

8. Not only that, a proper rehabilitation system should be practiced for offenders to adjust to society after release.

CONCLUSION

1. In conclusion, as stated above, there are a few reasons for the increasing crime rate, and several approaches to unravel it are suggested as well.

2. By analyzing the reasons thoroughly, appropriate solutions should be applied to sort out the problem.

3. In this way, the society can become a crime-free society.

PREVIOUS TEST

1. The crime rate nowadays is decreasing compared to the past due to advance technology which can prevent and solve a crime.
   Do you agree or disagree? (2018.)

2. Studies show that many criminals do not receive enough education. For this reason, people believe that the best ways to reduce crime is to educate them so they can find a job after being released. Do you agree or disagree?

3. It is often thought that the increase in juvenile crime can be attributed to violence in the media. Do you agree that this is the main cause of juvenile crime?
   What solutions can you offer to deal with this situation?

** 첨삭은 **ieltseasywriting.com**

A few countries punish the criminal with the death penalty. However, others think life imprisonment is a better punishment for crimes. What is your view?

ESSENTIAL VOCA

INTRODUCTION

범죄율	the crime rate
계속 증가하는 범죄율	the ever-increasing(ever-rising/ever-growing) crime rate
사법 제도	a justice(legal) system
집행	enforcement/execution
최고 형량	a maximum punishment(penalty)
사형	capital punishment/death penalty/execution/the punishment of death
중죄	a felony/a grave offense
종신형	life imprisonment/life in prison/life sentence
범죄자들	criminals/offenders/culprits
~에 대한 이목을 끄는 논란이 되다	become a high-profile controversy over
~에 대한 계속적인 논쟁이다	be an ongoing debate(controversy) over
비도덕적인	immoral/unethical
아무도 삶을 앗아갈 권리가 없다	no one has the right to take a life
~에 찬성하다	approve of/be for/be in favor of/agree with/be for~
~에 반대하다	be against/be not in favor of/disagree with~
자세히 설명하다	spell out/elaborate on/discuss in detail/explain in full detail

다음과 같이	as follows
다음은 이유들이다	the following are the reasons

BODY 1(disadvantages of capital punishment)

우선/먼저	first of all/above all/in the first place/first and foremost
다른 무엇보다도 가장 중요한 것은	most importantly/most important of all
분명한 증거가 없다	there is no clear-cut evidence that S+V
명백한 증거	a smoking gun/a clear-cut evidence/a hard proof
범죄를 저지르다	commit a crime/commit a criminal act
범죄를 근절하다	stamp out(root out/eradicate/uproot/deter) crimes
A가 B 하는 것을 억제하다	curb(deter/restraint/retard/inhibit) A from B
억제 수단으로써	as a deterrent
다시 말해서	in other words/to put it another way/that is/that is to say
사실상	in fact/in reality/as a matter of fact/actually/virtually
사형을 시행하다	implement(carry out/impose/conduct) the death penalty
비효율적이고 부정적인 결과들	ineffective and unfavorable consequences
전혀 효과가 없다	go nowhere/be unsuccessful/have no effect at all
중한 벌	a severe(heavy/intensive/grave) punishment
~에 관해서는	concerning/regarding/with respect to/as regards~
계획적인 범죄	a premeditated crime/a calculated crime
주의하다/조심하다	take precaution/be careful/be discreet
잡히지 않기 위해서	not to get caught/not to be taken/not to be arrested
덧붙여서	in addition to that/on top of that/furthermore/moreover
실제 사례들	real(actual) examples(cases/instances)
사형 반대자	capital punishment opponents(dissenters/objectors)
무죄인 사람들/유죄인 사람들	innocent people/guilty people
가능성이 있다	there is possibility(likelihood/probability) that S+V

부당하게 유죄선고를 받고 사형을 당하다	innocent people could be wrongly convicted and executed
범죄 문제를 해결하다	address(tackle/battle/sort out/solve) crime problems

BODY 2(life in prison)

사형 대신에	instead of(in place of/in lieu of) the death penalty
A에게 B를 선고하다	sentence A to B/condemn A to B
범죄자에게 종신형을 선고하다	sentence offenders to life in prison
사법당국	the law enforcement/the judicial authorities
범죄생활	a life of crime
극심한 고통	overwhelming(extreme/severe) distress(suffering/pain)
심하고 긴 고통	an intense and prolonged pain
겪다	undergo(go through/suffer from/experience)
남은 삶 동안 수감되다	be imprisoned for the rest of life
감옥에서 죄를 반성하다	reflect on the wrongdoing(sin) in prison
피해자들/희생자들	the victims
범죄를 두려워하여	for fear of crimes
외상 후 스트레스 장애를 겪다	struggled with(suffer from/undergo) severe post-traumatic stress disorder
과중한 처벌	a severe(heavy/intensive) punishment
법규에 따라	according to(in compliance with) the law(regulation)
법을 제정하다	legislate(make/enact/create) a law
법을 지키다	comply with(adhere to/abide by) the law
강화된 법	an enhanced(strengthened/intensified) law
강화하다	beef up/reinforce/strengthen/fortify/intensity
A를 실행하다	carry out(practice/implement/conduct) A/put A into practice(action)
벌금과 처벌의 강력한 시스템	the stricter system of penalties and punishments
강력한 법적 조치를 취하다	take a strong legal measure(step/action)
이러한 점에 있어서	in this respect/in this regard/in this sense/in this light

이러한 맥락에서/따라서	in this context/therefore/thus/as a result/consequently/hence
~보다는	rather than
설득력이 있는	compelling/reasonable/advisable/desirable/persuasive

CONCLUSION

결론적으로/요약하면	in conclusion/to conclude/to sum up
위에서 언급한 것처럼	as stated above/as mentioned above
모든 것을 고려할 때	all things considered
긴 안목에서/결국에는	in the long run/after all/in the end
~에 대한 최상의 해법	the best solution(answer/key) to+N
흉악한	atrocious/fierce/cruel/brutal
~때문에	on account of/because of/due to/owing to~
비효율적이고 부정적인 결과	ineffective and unfavorable consequences
가장 최상의	far and away the best/by far the best
고려하다	deem/consider/regard
이치에 맞다	make sense/stand to reason/be logical
최고 형량	a maximum punishment/a maximum penalty
범죄 없는 사회	a crime-free society

SENTENCE PRACTICE

INTRODUCTION

1. 사형이나 종신형 집행에 대한 계속적인 논쟁이 있어 왔다.

_____

_____

2. 많은 사람들은 심각한 중죄에 대한 처벌로써 사형에 찬성한다.

_____

_____

3. 그러나, 나는 그것이 비윤리적이고 아무도 삶을 빼앗을 권리가 없기 때문에 사형에 반대한다.

_____

_____

4. 다음의 문단에서, 나는 이유들을 자세히 설명하겠다.

_____

_____

BODY 1

1. 우선, 사형이 사람들이 범죄를 저지르는 것을 막을 수 있다는 분명한 증거가 없다.

_____

_____

2. 다시 말해서, 사형은 범죄에 대한 억제책으로서 적절한 처벌이 아니다.

_____

_____

3. 사실상 사형제도가 있는 나라들의 범죄율이 그것을 시행하지 않는 다른 나라보다 훨씬 높다.

_____

_____

4. 그것은 일부의 범죄자들은 죄를 범하기 전에 그들이 받을지도 모르는 처벌에 대해 거의 생각하지 않기 때문이다.

_____

_____

5. 계획적인 범죄에 있어서는, 범죄자들은 잡히지 않기 위해서 주의를 한다.

---

6. 덧붙여서, 무엇보다도, 무죄인 사람들이 부당하게 유죄를 선고받고 사형을 당할 가능성이 있다.

---

7. 실제로 사형 집행 후에 무죄가 증명되는 사례들이 있다.

---

8. 이것은 사형 반대자들이 계속 주장해 온 것이다.

---

9. 이러한 맥락에서, 나는 사형은 시행되면 안 된다고 믿는다.

BODY 2

1. 사형 대신에 당국은 범죄자에게 종신형 선고를 해야 한다.

---

2. 다시 말해서, 범죄들이 극심한 고통을 겪도록 그들은 남은 삶 동안 수감되어야 한다.

---

3. 그리고 감옥에서, 그들의 잘못된 행동으로 인해 생긴 피해자나 사회의 정신적 충격을 반성해야 한다.

---

4. 이 점에 있어서, 종신형은 강하고 긴 고통이며 그것은 사형보다 범죄자들에게 심한 처벌일 수 있다.

---

5. 그러므로, 당국이 사형보다 종신형을 집행하는 것이 설득력이 있다.

_____

_____

CONCLUSION

1. 결론은, 사형은 그의 비효율성과 부정적인 결과 때문에 흉악 범죄 처벌을 위한 최상의 해법은 아니다.

_____

_____

2. 모든 것을 고려할 때, 종신형이 최고 형량으로서 고려되어야 하는 것이 이치에 맞다.

_____

_____

ANSWER

INTRODUCTION

1. There has been an ongoing debate over the enforcement of either capital punishment or life imprisonment.

2. Many approve of the death penalty as an appropriate punishment for a serious felony.

3. However, I am against capital punishment since it is immoral and no one has the right to take a life.

4. In the following paragraphs, I will elaborate on the reasons.

BODY 1

1. Above all, there is no clear-cut evidence that capital punishment can deter people from committing crimes.

2. In other words, execution is not a proper punishment as a deterrent against crimes.

3. In fact, the crime rate in countries that impose the death penalty is still higher than that of the countries which do not implement it.

4. That is because some criminals rarely think about the punishment they would receive before they commit a crime.

5. Concerning a premeditated crime, the criminals take all precautions not to get caught.

6. In addition to that, most of all, there is the possibility that innocent people could be wrongly convicted and executed.

7. In reality, there are real examples where innocence was proved after execution.

8. It is what capital punishment opponents have constantly claimed.

9. In this context, I believe that the death penalty should not be enforced.

BODY 2

1. Instead of the death penalty, the authorities should sentence offenders to life in prison.

2. To put it another way, for criminals to undergo overwhelming distress, they should be imprisoned for the rest of their life

3. , and in prison, they must reflect on their wrongdoing and the trauma of the victims and society.

4. In this respect, life imprisonment is intense and prolonged pain, and it can be a more severe punishment to criminals than the death penalty.

5. It is, therefore, compelling for the authorities to implement a life sentence rather than capital punishment.

CONCLUSION

1. In conclusion, the death penalty is not the best solution to punishment for atrocious crimes on account of its ineffectiveness and unfavorable consequences.

2. All things considered, it makes sure that life imprisonment should be deemed as maximum punishment.

PREVIOUS TEST

1. Some people believe that not all criminals should be kept in prison, but that some of them should be allowed to do unpaid work to help the community. Do you agree or disagree?

2. Many criminals commit further crimes as soon as they released from prison. What do you think are the causes of this?
   What possible solutions can you suggest?

3. Many people believe that having a fixed punishment for all crimes is more efficient.
   What are the advantages and disadvantages of having a fixed punishment?

** 첨삭은 ieltseasywriting.com

Unit 4

The environment

1. Rain forest

2. Global warming

3. Waste problem

4. Zoo

1. Rain forest

It is true that rain forests are threatened by human activities. Some people say that rain forests can be destroyed for human development. However, others are against this opinion. What is your view?

ESSENTIAL VOCA

INTRODUCTION

열대 우림	rain forest/tropical rain forest
파괴하다/무너뜨리다	flatten/knock down/pull down/ruin/ravage/demolish
보존하다	conserve/protect/keep/preserve
동식물	fauna and flora/animals and plants
발전을 위해서	for the sake of(on behalf of/for the good of) advancement(development/progress/growth)
열대 우림의 손실	the damage(destruction/loss) of rain forest
심각한 문제	a critical(serious/severe) problem(concern/difficulty/trouble)
놀라운 속도로	at an alarming rate/at a startling rate
광범위한 영향	a far-reaching effect
중요한	essential/important/crucial/vital/significant
불가피한	inevitable/unavoidable/necessary/unpreventable
일반적인 사실이다	it is a common fact that S+V
A뿐만 아니라 B	B as well as A/not only A but also B
반면에	in contrast/by contrast/on the contrary/on the other hand
다음과 같이	as follows/in the following manner

BODY 1(the disadvantages of rain forest development)

우선	first of all/to begin with/first and foremost
생태계	the ecosystem/the ecological system
인간의 복지와 이익을 위해 이용되다	be exploited(used/employed) for human welfare and interest
새로운 식물과 동물 종들을 발견할 기회를 잃다	lose(miss) opportunities to fine new plant and animal species
무분별한 열대 우림의 파괴	the reckless(ruthless/heedless/careless/inconsiderable) destruction of rain forest
열대 우림의 손실	the loss of rain forest
덧붙여서	in addition to that/furthermore/moreover/what is more
해답을 얻다	hold(get) the answer/find(reach) a solution
불치병	incurable(permanent/terminal) diseases(illness)
환경적 저하	environmental degradation
산림 개간	forest clearing
벌목	logging/woodcutting
대규모의 산림벌채	large-scale(grand-scale/big-scale) deforestation
(나무 등을) 베어버리다	cut down(chop down/fall/log) trees
살아있는 모든 것들	all living things
먹이 사슬	the food chain
생명을 위협하는 수준	life-threatening levels
야생에서	in the wild
자연 서식지를 손상시키다	ravage(compromise/undermine/damage) natural habitats
동물들과 식물들의 서식지이다	be home to a large variety of animals and plants
멸종위기종의 서식지	the habitats of endangered species
멸종위기의 종들에 관한 한	as far as endangered species are concerned
멸종위기에 처해 있다	be in danger of extinction
동식물들을 멸종시키다	wipe out(die out/exterminate/kill off) fauna and flora(animals and plants)
파멸 직전에 있다	be on the brink(verge) of ruin
번식과 식물의 성장을 방해하다	hamper(retard/disturb) reproduction and vegetation growth
A를 위험에 빠뜨리다	put(place) A in danger/put(place) A at risk

위협받고 있다	be under treat/be at risk
~에 해롭다	be hazardous(harmful/injurious) to+Ⓝ
원자재들	raw materials/unprocessed materials
자원 고갈	the depletion(exhaustion) of resources
천연 자원을 다 써 버리다	deplete(use up) natural resources
자연 자원에 부담을 주다	put strain(burden) on natural resources
환경을 파괴하다	destroy(pollute/despoil) the environment
돌이킬 수 없는 손상	irreparable(irretrievable/irrecoverable) damage
열대 우림의 엄청난 감소는	the devastating decline of rain forest
~에 돌이킬 수 없는 손실을 가하다	inflict irreparable damage on~
녹는 빙하로 인한 해수면 상승	sea level rise caused by(generated by) melting glaciers
비참한 결과	dire(appalling/awful) consequences
지구 온난화에 기여하다	contribute to(make a contribution to) global warming
인간에 의해 발생된	brought on by(caused by/generated by/resulting from) human activities
열대식물	tropical vegetation
녹지 공간	green spaces
생물의 다양성 손실	the loss of biodiversity
원주민들	indigenous people/natives/aborigines
지구온난화를 막다	curb(deter/prevent/stop/fight against) global warming
A에게 B를 제공하다	provide(supply/furnish) A with B/provide(supply/furnish) B to A
~에 해로운 영향을 주다	have harmful(pernicious/detrimental) effects(influences/impacts) on~
환경에 심각한(중요한) 영향을 미치다	have serious(critical/vital) implications for the environment
~에 주요한 역할을 하다	play a major(key/leading/primary) role in~
이러한 이유들 때문에	for these reasons

BODY 2(the need of development)

다른 한편으로는	on the other hand/on the flip side/on the contrary
열대 우림의 손실	the loss of tropical rain forest
~이 분명하다	it is clear-cut(apparent/clear/obvious/undeniable) that S+V
~때문에	on account of(because of/due to/owing to)+Ⓝ
계속 증가하는 세계 인구	an ever-increasing world population
작물을 재배하다	cultivate(farm/grow) food crops
인간의 삶을 위해 공간을 만들다	make space for people's lives.
만약 ~이 아니라면	unless/if ~ not
인간의 무자비한 개발	human's heedless(thoughtless/indiscreet) development
인간의 복지와 이익을 위해	for human welfare and interest
열대 우림을 이용하다	exploit(make use of/utilize/use) rain forest

CONCLUSION

요약하자면	to sum up/in conclusion/to conclude
개발의 대가로	in exchange for development
손상시키다	compromise/hurt/damage/undermine
규제 없이	without regulation/without control
~에 위협을 가하다	pose(present) a threat to/threaten+Ⓝ
많은 양의 동식물	a significant amount of(a great deal of/a good deal of) plants and animals
멸종시키다	wipe out/die out/exterminate/cease to exist
잘 균형 잡힌 관계	a well-balanced relationship
보존	conservation/preservation/maintenance
환경과 개발사이의 균형을 유지하다	keep(maintain/hold) a balance between development and the environment
성장과 환경보호주의는 같이 갈 수 있다	growth and environmentalism can go hand in hand
현명하고 적절하게	wisely and properly/reasonably and appropriately

SENTENCE PRACTICE

INTRODUCTION

1. 열대 우림의 많은 부분이 인구의 팽창과 발전을 위한 공간을 만들기 위해 파괴되고 있다는 것은 일반적인 사실이다.

_____

_____

2. 일부는 열대 우림을 보존하는 것은 인간뿐만 아니라 동식물들에게 중요하다고 주장한다.

_____

_____

3. 반면에, 다른 사람들은 발전을 위해서 열대 우림을 어느 정도 손상시키는 것은 불가피하다고 주장한다.

_____

_____

4. 이 에세이는 다음과 같이 두 가지 의견을 고려할 것이다.

_____

_____

BODY 1

1. 우선, 열대 우림은 생태계를 위해서 보존되어야 한다.

_____

_____

2. 왜냐하면 그것은 현존하는 동식물뿐만 아니라 아직 발견되지 않는 종에도 서식지를 제공하기 때문이다.

_____

_____

3. 만약 열대 우림의 파괴가 일어나면, 사람들은 새로운 식물과 동물 종들을 발견하는 기회를 잃어버릴 것이다.

_____

_____

4. 그것은 불치병을 치료하는 데 해답을 가질 수 있다.

_____

_____

5. 이것에 덧붙여서, 무분별한 열대 우림의 파괴는 지구온난화를 초래한다.

_____

_____

6. 그것은 열대 우림의 엄청난 손실을 가져오는 감소는 환경에 돌이킬 수 없는 손상을 주고,

_____

_____

7. 기후 변화와 녹는 빙하로 인한 해수면 상승과 같은 심각한 문제들을 발생시키기 때문이다.

_____

_____

8. 이러한 이유들 때문에, 지구의 온난화를 막기 위해서 열대 우림을 보호하는 것이 아주 바람직하다.

_____

_____

BODY 2

1. 다른 한편으로는, 인간의 발전을 위해 열대 우림의 손실은 피할 수 없다.

_____

_____

2. 세계적으로 계속되는 인구 증가로 인해 인간을 위한 식량뿐만 아니라 더 많은 공간이 필요한 것은 분명하다.

_____

_____

3. 이러한 것을 위해, 세계에서 가장 큰 열대 우림인 아마존은 사람들의 삶을 위해 작물을 재배하고 공간을 만들기 위해 개발되고 있다.

_____

_____

4. 따라서 만약 그것이 열대 우림의 무분별한 파괴가 아니라면, 인간의 복지와 이익을 위해 그들은 이용될 수 있다.

_____

_____

CONCLUSION

1. 요약하자면, 열대 우림이 보호되어야 하지만 그들은 개발의 대가로 어느 정도 손상되고 있다.

_____

_____

2. 그러므로, 만약 열대 우림이 규제 없이 개발된다면, 동물과 식물에 위협을 받게 되고 결국에는 멸종될 수 있다.

_____

_____

3. 그러므로, 개발자들과 정부들은 개발과 보존 사이에서 현명하고 적절하게 균형을 유지해야 한다.

_____

_____

ANSWER

INTRODUCTION

1. It is a common fact that large parts of rain forests are being flattened to make space for human population expansion and development.

2. Some believe that conserving rain forests is essential for fauna and flora as well as human beings.

3. In contrast, others argue that for the sake of advancement, the damage of rainforests to some extent is inevitable.

4. This essay will consider both opinions as follows.

BODY 1

1. First of all, rainforests should be preserved for the ecosystem

2. since it provides habitats for undiscovered species as well as existing fauna and flora.

3. If the destruction of rainforest occurs, people will lose opportunities to find new plants and animal species.

4. That could hold the answer to the treatment of incurable diseases.

5. In addition to that, the reckless destruction of rainforests contributes to global warming.

6. It is because the devastating decline of rainforests inflicts irreparable damage on the environment

7. , giving rise to critical problems, including climate changes and rising sea levels generated by melting glaciers.

8. For these reasons, it is highly desirable to protect rainforests to curb global warming.

BODY 2

1. On the other hand, the loss of tropical rainforests is unavoidable for human progress.

2. It is clear-cut that not only more space but also food is needed for human beings, on account of the ever-increasing population worldwide.

3. For which the Amazon, the world's largest rainforest, has been developed to cultivate food crops and make space for people's lives.

4. Thus, unless it is the heedless destruction of the rainforests, they can be exploited for human welfare and interest.

CONCLUSION

1. To sum up, rainforests should be protected, though. They have been somewhat compromised in exchange for development.

2. Therefore, if rainforests are developed without restriction, it would pose a threat to significant amounts of plants and animals, which could wipe them out in the end.

3. In this context, developers and governments should keep a balance between exploitation and preservation wisely and appropriately.

PREVIOUS TEST

---

1. Rainforests are the lungs of the earth. Destruction of the world's forests amounts to death of the world we currently know. To what extent do you agree or disagree?

2. Deforestation caused by human activities is happening in many parts of the world, with serious results of the environment. What do you think can be done to solve this problem?

3. Deforestation is a serious problem, and it may lead to the extinction of animals and humankind. Do you agree or disagree with this statement?

** 첨삭은 **ieltseasywriting**.com

2. Global warming

Global warming is one of the most serious issues the world faces today. What are the causes of global warming and what measures can governments and individuals take to tackle the issue?

ESSENTIAL VOCA

INTRODUCTION

지구온난화	global warming
환경적 문제들	environmental challenges(problems/concerns/troubles)
놀라운 속도로	at an alarming(startling) rate(pace)
지난 십 년에 걸쳐서	over the past decade
중요한	critical/vital/important/significant/crucial
긴급한 사회적 문제	a pressing(urgent/burning) social issue
광범위한 영향	a far-reaching(extensive/widespread/wide-ranging) effect
몇 가지 원인들	a few(several/a couple of) culprits(reasons/causes/grounds)
해결책들	solutions/answers/keys/remedies
이 문제와 관련된	associated with(related to/linked to) this issue
정부 시책들/정책들	the government initiatives(policies)
분석하다/검토하다	analyze/examine

BODY 1(causes/effects)

지구온난화에 대한 근본적인 원인	the underlying(root/fundamental/primary) cause of global warming
과소비	overconsumption/excessive spending
과도한 포장	excessive packaging
일회용 상품	a disposable product(item)
과도한 자연 자원의 소비	the excessive consumption of natural resources
증가하는 차량의 수	the increasing number of vehicles(cars)
상황	circumstances/conditions/surroundings
이산화탄소(일산화탄소) 방출량	the quantity of carbon dioxide emissions(carbon monoxide)
이산화탄소를 배출하다/발생시키다	generate(produce/emit) carbon dioxide
탄소 배출량(온실효과를 유발하는 이산화탄소의 배출량)	carbon footprint
대기권에	in the atmosphere(air)
오존층의 파괴를 야기하다	induce(trigger/generate/provoke) the depletion(destruction) of the ozone layer
온실효과	the greenhouse effect
자외선	ultraviolet radiation
무더위/열 파	the heat wave
가속화된 기후 변화	an elevated level of climate change
기후 변화에 취약하게 되다	become vulnerable to climate change
해빙	melting/thawing
극지방의 만년설	polar ice-caps
극심한 기후 조건들로 특징화된 기후 변화	characterized by(marked by) extreme weather conditions
극심한 더위와 추위를 겪다	go through(undergo/experience/suffer) severe hot and cold
인구 과잉의 문제에 직면하다	face(confront/encounter) the problem of overpopulation
현재 상황	the status quo/the current situation/the existent circumstances
삼림 벌채	deforestation/logging/lumbering
열대 우림의 파괴	the destruction(devastation/demolition) of rain forest
(나무 등을) 베어 버리다	chop(cut) down trees/fall trees
천연 자원 고갈	the depletion(exhaustion) of natural resources

빈약한 자원	meagre(scarce) resources
천연 자원을 다 써 버리다	use up natural resources
오염시키다	pollute/contaminate
오염 물질을 방출하다	release(discharge/emit) pollutants(contaminants)
도시화	urbanization
사막화	desertification
후진국들	low-income(underdeveloped/undeveloped) countries
인간의 무자비한 개발	human's heedless(ruthless/cruel) development
인간이 만든 재앙들	man-made catastrophes(disasters/misfortunes)
인간이 초래한 지구온난화	human-induced(human-caused) global warming
인간의 활동들에 의한	brought on by(caused by/generated by/resulting from/driven by) human activities
규제 없이	without a regulation/without control
개발의 대가로	in exchange for development
위험 수준에 다다르다	reach an alarming level/be at dangerous level
자연 자원에 부담을 주다	put(place) strain on natural resources
기본적인 인권을 침해하다	threaten(infringe on) fundamental human rights

BODY 2(approaches)

그럼에도 불구하고	nonetheless/nevertheless/for all that/still
지구온난화를 둔화시키다	slow down(curb/stop/prevent/block/deter) global warming
개인적인 측면에서	as for(when it comes to/in terms of/in the case of) people(individuals)
스스로	of one's own accord/personally/for oneself/on one's own
대중교통의 이용	the use of public(mass) transportation
가스배출을 감소시키다	lessen(cut down on/cut back on) the discharge of gasses
화석 연료의 연소	fossil fuel combustion/burning fossil fuel
수소자동차	a hydrogen car
대체 에너지	alternative energy/renewable energy

화석연료와 같은 전통 자원	a conventional(traditional) source like fossil fuel
천연 자원을 손상시키다	compromise(undermine/deteriorate/damage) natural resources
천연 자원을 이용하다/활용하다	exploit(make use of/take advantage of/employ) natural resources
물품을 재활용하려 노력하다	make(exert) a great effort to recycle items
강력한 법규를 시행하다	implement(carry out/organize/conduct) strong(strict) regulations
보호 조치와 함께	in conjunction with(along with/coupled with) conservation measures
조치를 취하다	take action(steps/measures)
범법자에게 벌을 주다	inflict(impose) a penalty upon an offender
보조금을 주다	award a grant/subsidize/grant a subsidy
법규를 어기다	violate(break/infringe) a regulation
과중한 벌금형을 받다	incur(receive) a heavier(hefty) fine(penalty)
자연 보호구역	a nature conservation area/a natural reserve
(문제/상황 등에 대해) 다루다/해결하다	address/cope with/tackle/battle/combat
지구온난화를 둔화시키다	slow down(ease/relieve/lessen) global warming
지구온난화를 막다	curb(deter/stop/block) global warming
종결시키다/끝내다	put an end to(finish/wind up/bring an end to) global warming
주요한 역할을 하다	play a major(key/leading/primary) role in+Ⓝ

CONCLUSION

결론은	to sum up/to conclude/in conclusion
어느 정도	to some(a certain) degree(extent)/more or less/somewhat
지구온난화에 대한 주요한 원인	the major(primary/main) cause of global warming
제시된 실행 가능한 해결책	a feasible solution presented(shown/suggested/mentioned/proposed)
지구온난화에 맞서 싸우다(방지하다)	fight against global warming
관련된 단체들	organizations involved
~와 협력하다	team up with/cooperate with/collaborate with/work together with

SENTENCE PRACTICE

INTRODUCTION

1. 지구온난화는 지난 십 년간에 걸쳐 중요하고 긴급한 환경적인 문제가 되고 있다.

_____

_____

2. 지구온난화의 이면에는 몇 가지 원인들이 있고 이 문제에 대한 몇 가지 해결책들이 있다.

_____

_____

3. 이 에세이는 그들 원인들의 몇 가지를 분석하고 이 문제와 관련된 가능한 해결책들을 제안할 것이다.

_____

_____

BODY 1

1. 지구온난화의 주요한 원인들 중의 하나는 광범위한 인간 활동들이다.

_____

_____

2. 특히 과소비와 증가하는 차량들의 수는 이러한 현상에 대한 주요한 원인들이다.

_____

_____

3. 이러한 상황들은 탄소가스, 매연 그리고 해로운 화학물질들을 발생시킨다.

_____

_____

4. 이러한 것은 오존층 파괴와 지구온난화를 야기한다.

_____

_____

5. 오늘날, 지구는 또한 인구 과잉 문제에 직면하고 있고, 현재 상황은 전보다 훨씬 더 심각하다.

_____

_____

6. 이것에 덧붙여서, 개발을 위한 나무의 과다 벌채와 열대 우림의 파괴는 지구온난화를 발생시켜 왔다.

_____

_____

7. 극지방의 만년설의 해빙을 일으키고 홍수들, 가뭄들과 극심한 기후 조건들로 특징화된 기후 변화를 가져오고 있다.

_____

_____

8. 우리는 전 세계적으로 사람들이 기후 변화로 인한 극심한 더위와 추위를 겪는 것을 볼 수 있다.

_____

_____

9. 보여지는 것처럼, 몇 가지 원인들이 지구온난화에 상당한 영향을 준다.

_____

_____

BODY 2

1. 그럼에도 불구하고, 개인들과 정부가 지구온난화를 둔화시킬 수 있는 해결책들이 또한 있다.

_____

_____

2. 개인적인 측면에서 그들은 그들의 차 대신 대중교통을 이용해야 한다.

_____

_____

3. 이러한 것은 가스 배출을 감소시킬 수 있고 지구온난화를 지연시킬 수 있다.

_____

_____

4. 다른 조치로, 그들은 자연 자원과 환경을 손상시키는 일회용 상품을 사용하지 말아야 한다.

_____

_____

5. 정부 측면에서는, 그들이 취해야 할 주요한 조치는 지구온난화에 대해 시민과 기업들이 인식하게 하기 위해서 환경 캠페인을 실행하는 것이다.

_____

_____

6. 이와 같이, 정부는 그들에게 그들의 역할을 스스로 하게 할 수 있다.

_____

_____

7. 두 번째로, 정치 지도자들은 이 문제를 예방하고 종결시키기 위해서 강력한 법규를 만들고 시행해야 한다.

_____

_____

8. 만약 시민들과 기업들이 그 법규를 어긴다면, 그들은 과중한 벌금형을 받아야 한다.

_____

_____

9. 이런 방법들을 기반으로, 국민들은 지구온난화를 줄이고 억제하기 위해서 조치를 취해야만 한다.

_____

_____

CONCLUSION

1. 위에서 언급한 것처럼, 인간의 활동들과 개발들은 지구온난화의 주요한 원인들이다.

_____

_____

2. 그러나, 그것을 해결하기 위해 제시된 실행 가능한 해결 방법들이 있다.

_____

_____

3. 그러므로, 개개인들과 정부들은 지구온난화를 방지하고 맞서기 위해 서로 협력해야 한다.

_____

_____

ANSWER

INTRODUCTION

1. Global warming has been a critical and pressing environmental concern over the past decade.

2. There are several culprits behind global warming and a few solutions to the problem.

3. This essay will analyze some of these reasons and propose possible remedies associated with the issue.

BODY 1

1. One of the leading causes of global warming is far-reaching human activities.

2. In particular, overconsumption and the increasing number of vehicles are the key reasons for the phenomenon.

3. Those circumstances generate carbon gases, fumes and hazardous chemicals

4. , which induce the depletion of the ozone layer and global warming.

5. Today, the earth also faces the problem of overpopulation, and the status quo is far more serious than before.

6. Furthermore, the overcutting of trees and the destruction of rainforests for development have led to global warming

7. , bringing about the melting of the polar ice-caps, and triggering climate changes characterized by floods, drought and extreme weather conditions.

8. We can observe globally that people go through severe hot and cold generated by climate change.

9. As can be seen, a few factors have significant influences on global warming.

BODY 2

1. Nevertheless, there are also a couple of solutions for individuals and governments to slow down global warming.

2. As for people, they should use public transportation instead of their car.

3. This can lessen the discharge of gasses and delay global warming.

4. Another step is that they should not use disposable products that undermine natural resources and the environment.

5. In light of governments, the primary measures they should take are to carry out environmental campaigns to make citizens and companies aware of global warming.

6. With this, governments can have them play their role of their own accord.

7. Second, political leaders ought to make and implement strong regulations to prevent and put an end to this problem.

8. Provided that citizens and companies violate the regulations, they should incur a heavier fine.

9. Based on these ways, people and governments should take action to lessen and curb global warming.

CONCLUSION

1. As mentioned above, human activities and developments are the major sources of global warming.

2. However, there are feasible solutions presented to tackle it.

3. Thus, individuals and governments should team up with each other to prevent and fight against global warming.

PREVIOUS TEST

---

1. Nowadays, environmental problems are too big to be managed by individual persons or individual countries. In other words, it is international problems. Do you agree or disagree with this statement?

2. Some people argue higher taxes should be collected from industries causing higher industrial pollution, whereas others argue there are better ways to deal with it. Discuss both views and give your opinion.

3. Technology is a cause of environmental pollution. Some say that we should not use it to make our lives simple. Others believe that we should use it to tackle the problem. Discuss both views and give your own opinion.

** 첨삭은 **ieltseasywriting.com**

A great amount of waste is becoming a social problem. What should individuals and the government do to lessen waste? Suggest feasible solutions.

ESSENTIAL VOCA

INTRODUCTION

많은 양의 쓰레기	a great(enormous) amount of waste(trash/rubbish/garbage)
증가하는 쓰레기 양	an increasing(growing/rising) amount of waste
많은 사람들	a number of(plenty of/numbers of) people
다양한 종류의 쓰레기에 노출되다	be exposed to(get exposure to) various kinds of wastes
버리다/처분하다	throw away/discard/dispose of/get rid of/dump
무분별하게	indiscreetly/thoughtlessly/irrationally
인간의 활동에 의한	brought on by(caused by/generated by/resulting from) human activities
긴급한 사회적 문제	a pressing social issue
계속되는 사회적 문제	an ongoing(lasting) social concern
환경적 문제	environmental challenge(problem/concern/trouble)
제안들	suggestions/plans/proposals
(문제/상황 등에) 다루다/해결하다	address/resolve/cope with/deal with/sort out/settle/tackle/battle
확실하다/사실이다	it is certain that(it is true that/it is a fact that) S+V
야기하다/일으키다	give rise to(lead to/result in/bring about)+Ⓝ
제시하다	present/show/describe/explain/illustrate/discuss
다음과 같이	as follows

BODY 1(individuals)

개인에 대해 말하자면	when it comes to(in light of/regarding/concerning) individuals
분리하다	segregate/sort out/assort
물품들을 재활용하려 노력하다	make(exert) great(considerable) efforts to recycle items
폐지 재활용	recycling of waste paper
창조적 재활용	upcycling
그들이 할 수 있는 한	as much as they can
원자재를 보존하다	preserve(conserve/keep) raw materials
에너지를 절약하다	save(conserve) energy
A뿐만 아니라 B	not only A but also B/B as well as A
산업 쓰레기	industrial waste
방사능 폐기물	radioactive waste
쓰레기 소각장	a garbage incineration plant
쓰레기 매립지	a landfill/a reclaimed land(ground)
오염 물질들	pollutants/contaminants
오염시키다	pollute/contaminate
1회용 제품들	a disposable item
과도한 포장	excessive packaging
과도한 자연 자원의 소비	the excessive consumption of natural resources
비참한 결과	a dire(appalling/awful) consequence
특히	in particular/particularly/especially/specifically
썩는 쓰레기	biodegradable garbage(waste)
독성 쓰레기	toxic waste(garbage/rubbish)
쓸모 없는 전자 제품	useless(worthless/out of date) electronic devices
전자 쓰레기	e-waste/electronic waste(garbage)
중대한 문제가 되다	become a grave concern(problem/trouble)
알려진 것처럼	as it is known/admittedly/of course
독성 요소들	toxic components/poisonous substances

~에게 해를 주다	be harmful(hazardous/injurious) to~
한 가지 예로	for one thing/to cite one example/to give an example
사례들	cases/examples/instances
거주민들	residents/inhabitants/local people/natives
질병에 걸리다	contract(develop/come down with) diseases
~에 막대한 손해를 끼치다	wreak havoc with/take a toll on~
환경에 심각한 영향을 미치다	have a serious implication for the environment
환경에 돌이킬 수 없는 손상을 주다	inflict irreparable damage on the environment
파멸 직전에 있다	be on the brink(verge) of ruin
A를 위험에 빠뜨리다	put(place) A in danger/put(place) A at risk
따라서/그러므로	as a result/consequently/therefore/thus/hence/in this context

BODY 2(governments)

반면에	meanwhile/on the other hand/on the contrary/in contrast
~에 대한 대안	as an alternative(solution) to+Ⓝ
A에게 B를 제공하다	provide(furnish/supply) A with B/provide(supply/furnish) B to(for) A
적절한 시설과 교육	adequate facilities and instructions
환경 친화적인 시설	an environmentally friendly system/a eco-friendly system
예산을 ~에 투자하다	invest budget in~
시민/일반 대중	the public/citizens/the general public
광범위한 영향	a far-reaching(far-flung/extensive) effect
환경에 이롭다	be beneficial for the environment/be of benefit to the environment
가정용 쓰레기에 대한 조치를 취하다	take action(steps) against household waste
사람들에게 쓰레기를 줄이라고 권장하다	encourage people to reduce waste
법에 따라	according to the law/in compliance with the law
벌금 또는 처벌	fine(penalty) or punishment
범법자에게 벌금을 부과하다	inflict(impose) a penalty upon an offender

~을 희망하면서	in the hope that S+V
질적인 삶을 강화하다	enforce(improve/develop) the quality of life
공익광고와 같은 캠페인을 통해서	through campaigns like public service announcements
환경에 대한 인식을 높이다	raise the awareness(conscious) of the environment
이러한 목적을 달성하기 위해	to that end/to this end
가능성 있는 해법	a possible(practical/viable/feasible/workable) way
어느 정도	to some degree(extent)/more or less/somewhat
쓰레기를 줄이다	scale back(curtail/reduce/cut back on/cut down on) waste
~에 해로운 영향을 주다	have pernicious(harmful/detrimental/adverse) influences(impacts/effects) on~

CONCLUSION

결론은	in conclusion/to conclude/to sum up
위에서 언급한 것처럼	as stated above/as mentioned above
강력한 조치와 함께	in conjunction with(along with/coupled with) strong measures
주요한 역할을 하다	play a major(key/leading/primary) role in+Ⓝ
정부 시책/정책	the government initiatives(policies)
각자의 몫	respective share
책임감 있게	responsibly/reliably
바람직한	desirable/recommendable/preferable/compelling
~와 협력하다	team up with/cooperate with/work together with

STENTENCE PRACTICE

INTRODUCTION

1. 많은 사람들이 다양한 종류의 쓰레기에 노출되고 있다는 것은 확실하다.

_____

_____

2. 대부분의 쓰레기는 무분별하게 버려지고 이런 것들은 오염과 다른 환경적 문제를 발생시킨다.

_____

_____

3. 따라서, 증가하는 쓰레기 양은 긴급한 사회적 문제가 되고 있다.

_____

_____

4. 이 에세이에서, 정부와 시민들은 쓰레기 문제를 해결하기 위해서 무엇을 해야 하는지에 대한 제안들이 제시될 것이다.

_____

_____

BODY 1

1. 개인에 대해 말하자면, 그들은 많은 양의 쓰레기 문제를 해결하기 위해 무언가를 해야만 한다.

_____

_____

2. 우선, 그들은 할 수 있는 한 쓰레기를 분리하고 재활용해야 한다.

_____

_____

3. 쓰레기를 분리하고 물건들을 재활용하는 것은 에너지를 절약할 뿐만 아니라 제품들에 사용된 여러 종류의 원자재를 보존할 수 있다.

_____

_____

4. 특히, 대량의 전자 쓰레기는 중대한 문제가 되고 있으므로, 쓸모 없는 전자 제품은 더욱 주의해서 다뤄져야 한다.

_____

_____

5. 알려진 것처럼, 건전지 같은 독성 물질들은 누출될 때 사람의 건강을 해칠 수 있다.

_____

_____

6. 한 가지 예로, 중국에서 무분별하게 버려진 전자 제품 쓰레기 때문에 강이 오염이 되어서 주변 주민들이 피부병에 걸린 사례들이 있다.

_____

_____

7. 이 문제를 피하기 위해서 시민들은 전자 쓰레기를 분리하고 그것을 적절하게 폐기해야 한다.

_____

_____

BODY 2

1. 반면에, 정부는 시민들이 재활용을 하고 쓰레기를 버릴 수 있는 적절한 시설과 교육을 제공해야 한다.

_____

_____

2. 이러한 목적을 달성하기 위해서, 그들은 환경친화적인 시설을 만드는 데 예산을 투자해야 한다.

_____

_____

3. 그들은 또한 공익광고와 같은 캠페인을 통해서 쓰레기를 버리는 방법과 재활용의 필요성에 대한 시민들의 인식을 높여야 한다.

_____

_____

4. 쓰레기를 줄이는 다른 가능한 조치는 강력한 법규를 만들고 범법자에게 벌을 주는 것이다.

_____

_____

5. 만약 사람들이 쓰레기를 무분별하게 버리거나 재활용을 하지 않을 경우에, 그들의 행동은 환경에 치명적인 영향을 준다.

---

6. 그러므로, 법에 따라 벌금 또는 처벌이 필요하다.

---

7. 이러한 정책들은, 시민들에게 이 문제에 대한 심각성을 제시하고 그것을 어느 정도 쓰레기를 줄일 것이다.

CONCLUSION

1. 요약하면, 위에서 언급한 것처럼, 정부와 개개인들은 쓰레기 문제를 해결하기 위한 몇 가지 방법들이 있다.

---

2. 결과적으로 정부와 시민은 쓰레기 문제를 책임감 있게 다루기 위해서는 서로 협력하고 그들의 각자의 분담을 하는 것이 바람직하다.

ANSWER

INTRODUCTION

1. It is certain that a number of people have been exposed to various kinds of wastes.

2. Most trash is thrown away indiscreetly, which gives rise to pollution and another environmental challenge.

3. Thus, an increasing amount of waste has become a pressing social issue.

4. In this essay, suggestions on what governments and citizens should do to address the waste problem will be presented.

BODY 1

1. When it comes to individuals, they should do something to resolve the issue of an enormous amount of waste.

2. Above all, they have to segregate and recycle trash as much as they can.

3. Sorting out waste and recycling items not only save on energy, but also preserve some of the raw materials used on the products.

4. In particular, useless electric devices should be carefully handled as the large quantities of e-waste become a grave concern.

5. As it is known, toxic components like batteries harm people's health when they are leaked.

6. For one thing, there are some cases in China in which residents, living near a river polluted electronic waste discarded indiscreetly, contract skin diseases.

7. To avoid this problem, people should separate e-waste and dispose of them properly.

BODY 2

1. Meanwhile, governments should provide adequate facilities and instructions for the public to recycle and get rid of junk.

2. To that end, they should invest budget in building environmentally-friendly establishment.

3. They also raise the citizens' awareness of how to dump garbage and the necessity of recycling through campaigns like public service announcements.

4. Another possible way of reducing waste is to build strict regulations and inflict a penalty upon an offender.

Unit

4

The environment

5. In case people throw waste away thoughtlessly and do not recycle it, their behaviors have pernicious influences on the environment.

6. Thus, fine or punishment is necessary according to the law.

7. Those kinds of policies would present the seriousness of this issue to citizens and, to some extent, scale back waste.

CONCLUSION

1. To sum up, as stated above, there are several methods for governments and individuals to tackle the rubbish problem.

2. Consequently, it is desirable for governments and citizens to team up with each other and do their respective share in addressing the waste problem responsibly.

PREVIOUS TEST

1. Some people claim that not enough of the waste from homes is recycled. They say that the only way to increase recycling is for governments to make it a legal requirement. To what extent do you think laws are needed to make people recycle more of their waste?

2. Electronic waste has become a serious problem. Why is it a problem and how it can be solved?

3. Nowadays we are producing more and more rubbish. Why do you think this is happening? What can governments do to help reduce the amount of rubbish produced?

** 첨삭은 **ieltseasywriting**.com

4. Zoo

> Zoos have no longer purpose, so they should be closed. Do you agree or disagree?

ESSENTIAL VOCA

INTRODUCTION

동식물군	fauna and flora
생태계	the ecosystem/the ecological system
동물 애호가들	animal lovers(activists)
동물들을 위해	for the sake of(for the good of) animals
주장하다	claim/maintain/argue/discuss
유지하다	maintain/keep/preserve
전적으로/확실하게	strongly/truly/firmly/completely/to a great degree(extent)
동의하다	agree with/be in favor of/be for/approve of
장단점들	pros and cons/advantages and disadvantages/merits and demerits/strengths and weaknesses
(문제/상황 등에 대해) 다루다/해결하다	address/cope with/tackle/battle/combat/deal with
이유는 다음과 같다	the following are the reasons

BODY 1(agree)

우선	to begin with/first of all/first and foremost
사실은	in fact/in reality/as an matter of fact
부정적인 효과들	an adverse(negative/unfavorable) effect

진부한 생각	an outdated(old-fashioned/antiquated/stereotyped) idea
A에게 교육과 오락을 제공하다	provide(supply/furnish) A with education and entertainment
요즈음	nowadays/these days/recently/today
다른 종들과 비교하여	compared to(in comparison with/as compared with) other species
살아있는 모든 것들	all living things
관찰하다	look at/investigate/watch
현대 기술의 덕택으로	with the help of modern technology
고화질로 온라인 비디오를 통해	in high-definition(high-quality) through online videos
그러므로/따라서	in this context/thus/therefore/hence/as a result/consequently

BODY 2(agree)

사육 상태에	in captivity
제한된 공간의 제약을 받는다	be restricted(restrained) in limited spaces
자연 서식지	a natural habitat
야생동물 보호구역	a wildlife sanctuary/a wild-life preserve
자연 보호구역	a nature conservation area/a nature preserve
야생에서	in the wild/in the state of nature
야생성을 잃는 경향이 있다	tend to(have a tendency to/be inclined to/be liable to) lose wild nature
야생성을 손상시키다	compromise(undermine/damage) wild nature
거의 ~않다	hardly/scarcely/rarely/seldom
번식하다	propagate/breed/reproduce
야생동물의 번식과 식물의 성장을 방해하다	hamper(disturb) wildlife reproduction and vegetation growth
분류되다	be classified/be sorted
희귀동물들	a rare animal(beast)
멸종위기의 종들에 관한 한	as far as endangered(threatened) species are concerned
멸종위기에 처해 있다	be in danger of extinction/face the threat of extinction
멸종위기종의 서식지	the habitats of endangered species
위험에 처하거나 멸종에 가까워지고 있다	be close to being endangered or extinct

멸종시키다	wipe out/die out/exterminate
잘 보호된 서식지	a well-protected habitat
~에게 위협을 가하다	pose a threat to+Ⓝ/threaten+Ⓝ
초래하다/야기하다	lead to(result in/bring about/give rise to)+Ⓝ

BODY 3(agree)

동물을 악용하다/착취하다	exploit(make ill use of/abuse) animals
몇 가지 드문 경우에서	in some rare cases
영양 실조와 방치	malnutrition(insufficient nutrition) and neglect(negligence)
만일 그들이 더 이상 이익이 생기지 않을 경우	in case they are no longer of any value
그 이외에도	aside from that/other than that/besides
동물에 돌이킬 수 없는 손상을 주다	inflict irreparable damage on animals
동물의 권리를 침해하다	infringe on(violate/disregard) animal rights
생물권/생태계	ecological system/ecosystem/ecology/biosphere
주요한 역할을 하다	play a major(key/leading/primary) role in+Ⓝ
동물에 해로운 영향을 주다	have harmful(pernicious/detrimental) effects(influences/impacts) on animals

CONCLUSION

결론은	to conclude/in conclusion/to sum up
위에서 언급한 것처럼	as mentioned(stated) above
이런 점에서/이런 상황으로 볼 때	given that/in this sense/in this respect/in this regard
동물들을 위해서	for the sake of(for the good of/for the benefit of) animals
가치가 있다	deserve/merit/be worth
존재하다	exist/remain/keep
부정적인 효과들	adverse(negative/unfavorable) effects
조치를 취하다	take action(steps/measures)/carry out measures
동물원에 대한 대안으로서	as an alternative(solution) to zoos
정부 시책/정책	the government initiatives(policies)
바람직한/설득력 있는	advisable/desirable/preferable/favorable/persuasive/compelling

SENTENCE PRACTICE

INTRODUCTION

1. 동물원 유지에 대한 찬반이 오랫동안 논의되어 오고 있다.

_____

_____

2. 어떤 사람들은 동물원은 동물들을 위해 여전히 필요하다고 주장한다.

_____

_____

3. 그러나 나는 전적으로 주제에 동의한다. 다음은 내 입장에 대한 이유들이다.

_____

_____

BODY 1

1. 우선, 동물원이 아이들과 성인들에게 오락과 교육을 제공한다는 것은 진부한 사고이다.

_____

_____

2. 실제로, 과거에는, 동물들을 보는 것을 즐기기 위한 유일한 방법은 동물원을 방문하는 것이었다.

_____

_____

3. 그러나 요즈음, 현대 기술의 덕택으로, 동물들은 가정에서 접근할 수 있는 온라인 비디오들이나 웹사이트를 통해서 고화질로 보여질 수 있다.

_____

_____

4. 그러므로, 사람들은 이러한 즐거운 경험과 교육을 위해 동물원에 갈 필요가 없다.

_____

_____

BODY 2

1. 덧붙여서, 사육 상태에 있는 동물들은 제한된 공간에서 제약을 받는다.

_____

_____

2. 동물들의 자연 서식지들은 그들이 야생에서 자유롭게 뛰고 나무에 오를 수 있는 넓고 열린 공간이라는 것은 잘 알려진 사실이다.

_____

_____

3. 동물들이 동물원에 머물 때, 그들은 그들의 야생성을 잃는 경향이 있고 어떤 동물들은 사육 상태에서 번식을 거의 할 수 없다.

_____

_____

4. 한 가지 분명한 예는 판다이다. 그들은 갇혀 있을 때 번식이 느리다.

_____

_____

5. 이것은 판다의 개체 수를 급격하게 줄였고 이러한 것은 그들이 멸종위기 동물로서 분류되는 것으로 이어졌다.

_____

_____

BODY 3

1. 마지막으로 동물원의 동물들은 단지 인간의 이익을 위해서 악용되는 많은 경우가 있다.

_____

_____

2. 몇 가지 드문 경우에서, 동물들은 동물원에서 영양실조와 방치로 고통을 겪는다.

_____

_____

3. 그리고, 만일 더 이상 동물원에 이익이 생기지 않을 땐 일부는 다른 동물로 대체된다.

_____

_____

4. 그 외에도, 동물원에서 동물 공연을 위해, 조련사들은 그들을 훈련하기 위해서 동물들에게 고통을 준다.

_____

_____

5. 이러한 것은 동물의 기본적인 권리를 침해한다.

_____

_____

CONCLUSION

1. 요약하자면, 위에서 언급한 것처럼 동물원에서 동물을 보호하는 데 있어 많은 부정적인 효과들이 있다.

_____

_____

2. 따라서, 동물원은 존재할 가치가 없다.

_____

_____

3. 이런 점에서 정부와 동물원과 관련된 기관들은 동물들을 위해 적절한 조치를 취하는 것이 바람직하다.

_____

_____

ANSWER

INTRODUCTION

1. The pros and cons of maintaining zoos have been debated for a long time.

2. Some people claim that zoos are still necessary for animals.

3. I, however, strongly agree with this idea. The following are the reasons for my position.

BODY 1

1. To begin with, the opinion that zoos provide children and adults with entertainment and education is an out- dated idea.

2. In fact, in the past, the only way to enjoy looking at animals was to visit zoos.

3. Nowadays, though, with the help of modern technology, animals can be viewed in high definition through online videos and websites that can be accessed even at home.

4. In this context, people do not need to go to zoos for enjoyable experience and education.

BODY 2

1. On top of that, animals in captivity are restricted in limited spaces.

2. It is a well-known fact that the natural habitats are broad and open areas where they can run freely and climb trees in the wild.

3. When animals stay in zoos, they tend to lose their wild nature, and some animals can hardly breed in captivity.

4. One obvious example is pandas. They are slow to reproduce when in captivity.

5. It dramatically lowered the population of panda, which led to them classified as an endangered species.

BODY 3

1. Finally, there are many cases in which animals kept in zoos are merely exploited for human's profits.

2. In some rare cases, animals undergo malnutrition and neglect in zoos

3. , and in case they are no longer of any value, some are replaced by other animals.

4. Aside from that, for animal performances in zoos, trainers inflict pain on animals to train them.

5. Those things infringe fundamental animal rights.

CONCLUSION

1. To sum up, as mentioned above, there are many adverse effects of keeping animals in zoos.

2. Therefore, zoos do not deserve to exist.

3. Given this, it is advisable for governments and organizations involved in zoos to take action for the sake of the animals.

PREVIOUS TEST

1. International animal rights groups argue it is wrong to use and kill animals for the benefit of human beings. Do you agree or disagree with this statement?

2. Both governments and individuals are spending vast amounts of money protecting animals and their habitat. This money could be better spent dealing with fundamental issues in society such as poverty and health care.
To what extent do you agree?

** 첨삭은 **ieltseasywriting.com**

Culture

1. Online shopping

Most people believe that online shopping is better and more enjoyable than going to shopping centres. Do you agree or disagree?

ESSENTIAL VOCA

INTRODUCTION

소비	consumption/spending
증가하고 있다/감소하고 있다	be on the rise(increase)/be on the decrease(decline)
인터넷의 도래로	with the advent of the Internet
인터넷상에서	on the Internet/online
온라인 쇼핑	online shopping/e-shopping/shopping on the Internet
일반 상점들	offline shopping malls/general malls/brick and mortar shops
많은 소비자들	plenty of(a slew of/a number of) customers(shoppers/consumers)
물건을 구입하는 방법은	the method of purchasing products
상품들	products/items/goods/commodities
구매하다	shop/buy/purchase/make a purchase
즐거운 경험	pleasant(delight/entertaining/enjoyable) experience
A에게 B를 제공하다	provide(supply/furnish) A with B/provide(supply/furnish) B to(for) A
동의하다	be for/be in favor of/agree with/support
전자/후자	the former(the one)/the latter(the other)

BDOY 1(advantages)

우선	to begin with/first and foremost/first of all
온라인 쇼핑과 관련해서	concerning(regarding/as regards/as respects) online shopping
편리함과 비용 절감을 제공한다	provide(offer/give) convenience and cost saving
쇼핑몰에 가다	travel(go) to a shopping mall
시간과 노력을 절약하다	save time and effort(time and care)
가치 있는	worthwhile/worth/valuable/of value
A가 B 하는 게 가능하다	enable A to B/allow A to B
상품 가격 측면에서	when it comes to(in light of/with respect to) the price of products
저렴한 가격에	at a low price/at an affordable price
그러한 가격들 때문에	on account of(due to/because of/owing to) those prices
할인 가격으로	at a bargain(reduced/discounted) price
파격 세일하다	be on special offer
값을 흥정하다	haggle about the price
비용 절감	cost saving(cutting)
시간과 경비를 줄이다	curtail(cut down on/cut back on/reduce) time and expense
투자비와 유지비	the cost of investment and maintenance
상품과 비교하여	compared to(in comparison with/as compared with) products
때때로	at times/sometimes/once in a while/now and then/on and off
다양한 상품들	all types of(all kinds of/all sorts of) products(items/goods)
중고품	second-hand goods/used items
신상품들	brand-new products
최신상품	the latest(newest) products
시장에 출시하다	release(launch/introduce) into the market
주저함이 없이	without any hesitation
구입하다/사다	make a purchase/buy/purchase
필요 없는 상품들	unnecessary items(goods)
상점 내 쇼핑	in-store shopping(purchasing)

바쁜 일상생활에서 벗어나다	escape from the hectic daily routines
상품을 물리적으로 사기 전에 검토하다	physically investigate(examine) the goods before purchase

BODY 2(advantages)

반면에	on the flip side/on the other hand/in contrast/by contrast
인터넷의 덕택으로	with the help of the Internet/thanks to the Internet
일로 바쁘다	be tired up with(be busy with) work
맞벌이 가정	a double-income family/two-carrier family
모든 연령층의 소비자들	consumers of all ages
노인들	the elderly/elderly people/senior citizens/the aged
장애요인들	obstacles/obstacle concerns(factors)
신체적 제약들	physical limitations(restrictions/restraints)
신체 장애인들	the physically challenged(disabled)/disabled people/the disabled
취약한 사람들	the vulnerable/vulnerable people
~에 취약하다	be vulnerable to+Ⓝ/be susceptible to+Ⓝ
~을 하지 않을 수 없다	cannot but+v/cannot help+~ing/cannot choose but+Ⓥ
쇼핑에 도움이 되다	be of help(be helpful) to shopping
편리한 쇼핑 환경	convenient shopping environment(surroundings/circumstances)
즐겁고 편안한 쇼핑 경험	an enjoyable and comfortable shopping experience
고가의 제품들	high-end(high-priced/costly/pricey) products
집으로 배달하다	deliver(send) products to house
소비자의 문 앞까지	to the shopper's doorstep
신속 배달 서비스	immediate(express) delivery services
완벽한 서비스	impeccable(complete) service
다양한 상품에 접근 가능하다	be accessible(reachable/handy) to a range of products
가상 쇼핑	virtual shopping
개선된 생활수준	the improved(enhanced) standard of living/the improved living standard

사람의 삶을 개선시키다	better(improve) people's lives
소비자들의 필요를 맞추다	cater to the needs of consumers
구매에 만족하다	be satisfied with a purchase
야기하다/초래하다/일으키다	give rise to(lead to/result in/bring about)+Ⓝ
~하는 사실에도 불구하고	despite the fact that S+V
~에 상당한 영향을 끼치다	have a significant(considerable/great/broad) effect on~
~에 긍정적인 영향을 끼치다	have a positive(affirmative/favorable) influence(effect/impact) on~
따라서/그러므로	therefore/thus/hence/in this context/as a result/consequently

CONCLUSION

결론은	to sum up/in conclusion/to conclude
위에서 언급한 것처럼	as stated above/as mentioned above
모든 것을 고려할 때	all things considered/taking all things into account(consideration)
~와 더불어	coupled with/along with~
시간과 경비를 줄이다	curtail(cut down on/cut back on/lessen/diminish) time and expense
~할 것 같다	be likely to~
이로운	beneficial/helpful/advantageous
성공과 인기	success and popularity(public interest)

SENTENCE PRACTICE

INTRODUCTION

1. 인터넷의 도래로 세계 곳곳의 사람들은 온라인에서 쇼핑을 해 오고 있다. 물건을 구입하는 이 방법은 사람들에게 많은 장점들을 제공한다.

_____

_____

2. 그러나 많은 소비자들은 일반 상점이 여전히 더 많은 즐거움을 준다고 믿는다.

_____

_____

3. 나는 다음의 이유 때문에 전자에 동의한다.

_____

_____

BODY 1

1. 우선, 인터넷을 통한 쇼핑은 편리함과 비용 절감을 소비자들에게 제공한다.

_____

_____

2. 온라인 쇼핑객들이 쇼핑몰까지 갈 필요가 없기 때문에, 그들은 온라인에서 쇼핑할 때 많은 시간을 절약할 수 있다.

_____

_____

3. 그것은 소비자들에게 다른 활동을 하는 것과 그들의 시간을 더 가치 있는 일에 보내는 것을 가능하게 한다.

_____

_____

4. 상품의 가격적인 면에서, 온라인 쇼핑몰은 상품들을 합리적인 가격 또는 때때로 일반 상점의 상품과 비교될 때 훨씬 더 낮은 가격에 상품을 제공한다.

_____

_____

5. 이것은 온라인 쇼핑몰 소매상들이 투자비와 온라인 상점 유지비를 덜 쓰기 때문이다.

_____

_____

6. 그러한 가격들 때문에, 일부의 소비자들은 상점에서 물건을 조사한 후 온라인에서 그 물건을 저렴한 가격에 구입한다.

_____

_____

BODY 2

1. 더욱이, 온라인 쇼핑은 노인들과 장애인들과 같은 취약한 사람들에게 몇 가지 이점들을 준다.

_____

_____

2. 육체적 조건 때문에, 그들은 쇼핑몰에서는 편안하게 쇼핑할 수가 없다. 거기에는 차별과 신체적 제약과 같은 많은 장애들이 있다.

_____

_____

3. 인터넷의 덕택으로, 그들은 그들이 구입을 원하는 물건을 선택하기 위해서 단지 마우스와 키보드만 필요하다.

_____

_____

4. 이것은 즐겁고 편안한 쇼핑 경험을 야기한다.

_____

_____

5. 그러한 이유들로, 온라인 쇼핑은 특히 노인들과 장애를 가진 사람들에게 유용하다.

_____

_____

CONCLUSION

1. 모든 것을 고려할 때, 시간과 경비를 줄이는 것과 더불어, 온라인 쇼핑은 오프라인 쇼핑보다 민감한 고객들을 포함한 모든 소비자들에게 훨씬 더 이롭다.

_____

_____

2. 그러한 이유들로, 온라인 쇼핑몰의 성공과 인기는 계속될 것 같다.

_____

_____

ANSWER

INTRODUCTION

1. With the advent of the Internet, people around the world have been shopping online. This method of purchasing products provides people with many advantages.

2. However, many consumers believe that offline shopping malls still offer more pleasant experiences.

3. I am for the former for the following reasons.

BODY 1

1. To begin with, shopping via the Internet provides convenience and cost saving to customers.

2. As online shoppers do not have to travel to shopping malls, they can save a lot of time and effort when shopping online.

3. It enables consumers to do other activities and spend their time on more worthwhile work.

4. When it comes to the price of products, online shopping malls supply items at a reasonable cost or at times, at an even lower price compared to products in brick-and -mortar shops.

5. This is because online retailers spend less on the cost of their investment and online store maintenance.

6. On account of those prices, some customers make a purchase of items online at low prices after examining them in real stores.

BODY 2

1. Furthermore, online shopping has several advantages to the vulnerable like the elderly and the disabled.

2. Due to their physical condition, they are unable to shop comfortably in shopping malls where there are many obstacles, including discrimination and physical limitations.

3. With the help of the Internet, they need only their keyboard and mouse to choose items they wish to buy

4. , which bring about an enjoyable and comfortable shopping experience.

5. Like this, online shopping is useful especially for seniors and those with disabilities.

CONCLUSION

1. All things considered, coupled with curtailing time and expense. Online shopping is much more beneficial for all customers including sensitive shoppers than offline shopping.

2. For those reasons, online shopping malls are more likely to continue their success and popularity.

PREVIOUS TEST

1. Online shopping is increasing dramatically. How could this trend affect our environment and the kinds of jobs required?

2. Shopping is the favorite pastime for most of the young people. Why do you think is that? Do you think they should be encouraged to do some other useful activities?

3. In the past, shopping was a routine domestic task. Many people nowadays regard as a hobby. To what extent do you think this is a positive trend?

** 첨삭은 **ielteasywriting.com**

Some people say that advertising encourages us to buy things that we do not really need. Others say that advertisements tell us about new products that may improve our lives. What is your view?

ESSENTIAL VOCA

INTRODUCTION

인터넷의 도래로	with the advent of the Internet
광고	advertisement/advertising/commercial
광고의 목적	the purpose of advertisement
광고에 대해서	with reference to(concerning/regarding/as regards) advertisement
넘쳐나는 광고	a flood of advertisement/overflowing advertisement
이목을 끌다	have a high profile
피할 수 없는 사실	an inescapable(unavoidable/inevitable) fact
다양한 상품 정보	a broad(whole/great/wide) range(variety/diversity) of product information
과도한 소비	excessive spending(consumption)/immoderate spending
긍정적인	positive/affirmative/bright/favorable/beneficial
부정적인 측면들	negative(minus/adverse/unfavorable) aspects(sides/respects/factors)
주요한 원인	the main(primary/chief/major) cause(reason/culprit)
주장하다	argue/claim/state/maintain/assert/voice
~에 대해 상세히 말하다	talk at length about/spell out/elaborate on/explain in full detail

BODY 1(positive factors)

우선	first and foremost/to begin with/first of all
긍정적인 측면	on the bright(positive) side
인터넷의 영향 정도/범위	the extent of the Internet influence
상품과 서비스에 대한 정보를 주다	give information on products and services
A뿐만 아니라 B도	B as well as A/not only A but also B
매력적인 광고	appealing(charming/attractive) advertisement
유익하고 흥미로운 광고들	informative and interesting advertisements(ads)
특수 효과와 매력적인 영상	a special effect and attractive visual
배경음악과 함께	with background music
소비자가 구매하도록 자극하다	stimulate(encourage/induce) consumers to buy
매우/아주/몹시	highly/extremely/greatly
정보의 전달	the dissemination of information
귀중한 정보	invaluable(priceless) information
~에 대한 다양한 정보를 주다	give a broad(wide/great) range(variety) of information on~
예를 들면	for instance/for example/for one thing/to give(take) an example
계획하다	make a plan/plan/work out a plan
관광지를 알아보다	find out(figure out/look into) travel destinations
여행 회사	a travel(tourist) agency
여행 경비	traveling expenses(charges/expenditures)
특징을 알아보다	figure out(find out/look into) a feature(character/distinction)
많은 노력을 하다	make(considerable/great) efforts//exert great efforts/put in a lot of work
시간이 걸리고 비용 면에서 비효율적인	time-consuming and cost-ineffective
결국 구입하다	end up making a purchase
구매를 야기하다/초래하다	bring about(result in/give rise to/lead to) a purchase

BODY 2(negative factors)

그에 반하여	on the other hand/on the contrary/on the flip side
부인할 수 없다	there is no denying that(it is certain that/it is undeniable that) S+V
A가 B 하는 것을 권장하다	encourage A to B
과도한 소비	excessive(immoderate) spending(consumption)
원하지 않은 상품들	unwanted items(products/goods)
필요 없는 상품들	unnecessary(needless/unneeded) products(items)
구매하다	make a purchase/purchase/buy
매우 구매하고 싶다	be keen to(be eager to/be anxious to/be dying to) purchase
신상품들	brand-new products
시장에 출시하다	release(launch/introduce) into the market
상품 충성도	brand loyalty
상품 인지도를 높이다	raise brand awareness
부가기능	an additional(extra/further) function
~와 비교하여	compared to/as compared with/in comparison with~
광고판	a billboard(signboard)
눈길을 사로잡는 헤드라인	attention-grabbing(eye-catching) headline
외설적이고 선정적인 장면	obscene and suggestive(sexual) scenes
미디어 검열	media censorship(monitoring)
미디어 교육 프로그램	a media literacy program
(광고 목적으로) 특정 상품을 영화나 드라마에 노출시키는 것/간접광고	product placement
광고 방송 시간	commercial break
공익광고	public service announcement(advertisement)
과잉광고	excess(exaggerated) advertisement
허위광고	false(fake) advertisement
해로운 물품에 대한 광고 금지	a ban on advertisements of harmful products
건강에 위험을 가하다	pose treats to(threaten) health conditions
최고 시청률 시간대에	in prime time

드라마 사이 광고 시간	commercial break during a soap opera
구매하도록 유혹받다	be lured into(be attracted to) purchase
광고에 의해 시달리다	be hassled by(be troubled by) commercial
유행하고 있다	be in fashion/be popular/be in vogue
유튜브에서 입소문이 나다	go viral on YouTube
청소년	adolescents/teens/teenagers
유명한 사람	a high-profile figure/a celebrity
연예인들	entertainers/celebrities
광고에서의 유명인사의 지지	celebrity's endorsement in advertising
TV광고에 출연하다	star(appear) in TV advertisements
과한 광고비	the high cost of advertisement
고가의 TV광고	expensive TV ads(commercials)
소비자 부담	consumer's burden(expenses)
~하는 사실에도 불구하고	despite the fact that S+V
그러므로/따라서	therefore/consequently/in this context/thus/hence

CONCLUSION

요약하자면	to sum up/to conclude/in conclusion
최종적인	once and for all
A를 고려하다	take A into consideration(account)/consider A
A에게 긍정적인 영향을 주다	have(exert)(positive/affirmative/favorable) influences(impacts/effects) on A
어떠한 경우에도	under any circumstances
단점들을 줄이다	cut down on(cut back on/reduce/lessen/curtail) drawbacks(demerits/negative factors)
훨씬 ~할 것 같다	be far(much) more likely to~
이치에 맞다/합리적이다	make sense/stand to reason/be logical
현명하고 적절하게	wisely and adequately/reasonably and appropriately

SENTENCE PRACTICE

INTRODUCTION

1. 현대사회에서 광고들은 사람들의 삶 속에 넘쳐나고 있다. 그리고 이것은 피할 수 없는 사실이다.

_____

_____

2. 어떤 사람들은 광고들이 다양한 상품정보를 제공한다고 믿는다.

_____

_____

3. 하지만 다른 사람들은 광고들은 과도한 소비 습관을 키운다고 주장하다.

_____

_____

4. 이 에세이에서, 나는 광고의 긍정적인 그리고 부정적인 두 측면을 자세히 설명하겠다.

_____

_____

BODY 1

1. 무엇보다 먼저, 광고의 목적은 기존의 것뿐만 아니라 새로운 상품과 서비스들에 대한 정보를 주는 것이다.

_____

_____

2. 이것은 소비자들에게 상품들을 사도록 자극한다.

_____

_____

3. 예를 들면, 많은 사람들은 그들의 휴가 동안 해외여행을 계획한다.

_____

_____

4. 그들은 여행 회사의 광고를 통해서 다른 관광지를 알아 볼 수 있고, 그것은 그들이 여행비용과 같은 정보를 얻는 것을 가능하게 한다.

_____

_____

5. 광고가 없다면, 구매자들은 어떠한 새로운 상품들이 만들어졌는지 그리고 그들이 가지고 있는 특성이 무엇인지를 알아내는 데 많은 노력을 해야 한다.

_____

_____

6. 하지만, 다양한 상품의 종류를 안다는 것은 쉽지 않다.

_____

_____

7. 덧붙여서, 이 과정은 시간이 걸리고 비용 면에서 비효율적이다.

_____

_____

8. 그러므로, 광고들은 정보의 전달과 관련해서 긍정적인 면을 가지고 있다.

_____

_____

BODY 2

1. 반면에, 광고들이 소비자에게 물건이 필요하지 않을 때에도 물건을 사도록 권장하는 것은 부인할 여지가 없다.

_____

_____

2. 이유는 광고들은 소비자들이 필요 없는 상품을 구입할 만큼 충분히 눈길을 끌기 때문이다.

_____

_____

3. 휴대폰을 예로 들어보자, 새 모델들은 전에 것과 비교하여 몇 가지의 부가적인 기능을 가지고 시장에 종종 출시된다.

_____

_____

4. 그러나, 시각적으로 매력적인 광고 때문에, 사람들은 그들의 휴대폰이 여전히 잘 작동한다는 사실에도 불구하고 새 것으로 바꾸고 싶어 한다.

_____

_____

5. 이러한 맥락에서, 구매자들은 광고 때문에 필요하지 않은 상품들을 사는 데 쉽게 유혹받는다.

_____

_____

CONCLUSION

1. 요약하자면, 이러한 모든 것들을 고려할 때, 비록 부정적인 효과들을 가지고 있지만 광고는 훨씬 더 긍정적인 영향을 소비자들에게 주는 것 같다.

_____

_____

2. 따라서, 소비자들이 광고를 현명하고 적절하게 이용하는 것이 이치에 맞다.

_____

_____

ANSWER

INTRODUCTION

1. Advertisements in modern society are overflowing in people's lives, and this is an inescapable fact.

2. Some people believe that ads offer a broad range of product information.

3. Others, however, argue that advertisements develop excessive spending habits.

4. In this essay, I will elaborate on both positive and negative aspects.

BODY 1

1. First and foremost, the purpose of advertisement is to give information not only on existing products or services but also on new ones.

2. It stimulates consumers to make a purchase.

3. For instance, many people plan to travel abroad during their holiday.

4. They find out different travel destinations through a travel agency advertisement which enables them to obtain information, including traveling expenses.

5. Without ads, buyers have to make considerable efforts to see what kinds of new items are produced and what features they have

6. , but it is not easy to be aware of various kinds of information about products.

7. Additionally, this process could be time-consuming and cost-ineffective.

8. Therefore, advertisements have a positive side regarding the dissemination of information.

BODY 2

1. On the other hand, there is no denying that advertisements encourage consumers to purchase new items even when they do not need it.

2. The reason is that commercials are eye-catching enough for customers to buy unnecessary products.

3. Take for example mobile phones. New models are often released into the market with just a few additional functions compared to the previous one.

4. However, on account of visually attractive advertisements, people are keen to change their phone to the new one despite the fact that their phone is still working well.

5. In this context, buyers are easily lured into unneeded items due to advertising.

CONCLUSION

1. To sum up, taking all these points into consideration, advertising, although having adverse effects, is far more likely to have favorable influences on consumers.

2. Consequently, it makes sense for consumers to use advertisements wisely and adequately.

PREVIOUS TEST

1. Companies use a variety of methods to improve the sales of their products. What are those methods? Which is the most effective method?

2. Companies spend millions each year on advertising online, in magazines and on billboards. These adverts can encourage people to buy goods that they do not really need. What do the positive and negative effect of consumerism? (2018.)

3. Many people buy products that they do not really need and replace old products with new ones unnecessarily. Why do people buy things they do not really need? Do you think this is a good thing?

** 첨삭은 **ieltseasywriting.com**

3. Traveling

People are traveling to other countries more than before. What are the advantages and disadvantages of traveling abroad?

ESSENTIAL VOCA

INTRODUCTION

최근에	In recent years/in recent times/nowadays/these days
사례들	instances/examples/cases
계속 증가하는 관광객	the ever-increasing(ever-growing/ever-rising) number of travelers
많은 관광객들	plenty of(a number of/a lot of/a load of) tourists
증가하고 있다	be on the rise(increase)
일반화되고 있다	become commonplace(common/general)
생활 수준	a standard of living/the living standard/the level of living
해외여행	overseas(international) traveling/traveling abroad(overseas)
해외여행을 가다	travel overseas(abroad)/leave(go) on a trip overseas/travel to other countries
관광객들	holidaymakers/tourists/travelers/visitors
교통	transportation/traffic/transport
저가 항공	budget airlines(low cost carriers)
다른 나라의 문화와 역사	the culture and history of other nations
A가 B 하는 것을 가능하게 하다	enable(allow) A to B
어려움을 겪다	go through(suffer/experience/undergo) difficulties(concerns/troubles)
부정적인 요인들	adverse(negative/minus/unfavorable) factors

단점들	drawbacks/disadvantages/negative factors/demerits
장점들	advantages/merits/benefits/positive factors
제시하다	present/explain/express/illustrate

BODY 1(positive factors)

몇 가지 이점들	several(a couple of/a few) benefits
부인할 수 없다	it is undeniable that(there is no denying that) S+V
시야를 넓히다	broaden one's horizons(outlook/views)
보람 있는(값진) 경험	a rewarding(valuable/worthy) experience
다양한 경험들	a broad(whole/great/wide) range(variety) of experiences
풍부한 경험(자원/지식/정보)	a wealth of experience(resources/knowledge/information)
즐거운 경험	an enjoyable(amusing/delightful) experience
유익한 경험	an enlightening(instructive/beneficial) experience
직접적인 경험을 갖다	get first-hand(hand-on/direct) experience
관심사의 영역을 넓히다	expand(broaden/widen/enlarge) the range of interest
새로운 생각들과 많은 지식을 접하다	come across(understand/experience) novel ideas and much knowledge
여행을 통해 에너지를 재충전하다	recharge energy(get refreshed) though traveling
짧은 휴식을 갖다	take(have) a short break
일상생활에서 벗어나다	escape from your daily routine/get out of everyday life
삶의 질	the quality of life
여행을 통해서 편견을 버리다	cast away(throw away/remove) prejudice(bias) through traveling
고정관념을 버리다	get rid of stereotype(fixed idea)
가족과 떨어져 있다	be away from family
여행을 통해서 자립을 배우다	learn independence through traveling
자립심을 기르다	cultivate(develop/form/keep/raise) self-reliance
스스로	by oneself/alone/on one's own
때때로	at times/once in a while/sometimes/now and then

예상하지 못한 상황이나 비상상황	unforeseen(unexpected/unpredicted) circumstances or emergencies
세계에 대한 시각을 넓히다	widen the perspective(point of view/outlook) of the world
문화적으로 받아들일 수 있는	culturally acceptable
이국적인 문화	exotic(foreign) culture
관광지들	tourist destinations(attractions/spots)
관광에 기반을 둔 경제	tourism-oriented economy
관광산업을 촉진시키다	boost(galvanize/develop/enhance/facilitate) tourism
지역 문화를 되살리다	reinvigorate(revive) local culture
매우 다양한 지역 특산물	a wide(broad) range of local crafts
돈을 잘 쓰는 여행객들	high-spending tourists
관광객을 끌어들이다	attract(draw) tourists
국가적인 이익	national benefits(interests)
관광산업을 통해서 경제적 침체를 벗어나다	get out of an economic downturn(depression) through tourism
충분한 수익	sufficient(enough/plenty of) income
수익성이 있는 산업	lucrative(profitable/productive/advantageous) industry
수익을 창출하다	generate(create) revenues(profits)
수익을 거두다	reap benefits/bring in revenues/make profits
지속 가능한 관광산업/환경친화적인 관광산업	sustainable tourism/environmentally-friendly tourism
생태관광산업	the ecotourism(eco-tourism) industry
관광산업을 통해 긴장을 완화하다	alleviate(lessen/ease/relieve) tension through tourism
~에 긍정적인 영향을 준다	have(exert) positive(affirmative/beneficial) effects(influences/impacts) on~

BODY 2(negative factors)

이에 반해서	on the contrary/on the other hand/on the flip side
우선	for one/most of all/first of all/above all
시간과 비용과 더불어	coupled with(along with) time and expense
많은 돈	a great amount of(a good deal of/large sums of) money/large quantities of money

Unit
5
Culture

여행 경비	traveling expenses(spending/costs)
재정적 부담	financial strain(burden/pressure)
~에게 무거운 부담을 주다	impose(give) a heavy burden on(to)~
거처/숙소	accommodation/staying
어려움을 겪다	experience(go through/suffer from/undergo) difficulties
보수적인 지역	a conservative(old-fashioned) region(area)
지역주민들과 마찰을 빚다	have a conflict with(make trouble with) local people(residents)
인종차별	racial discrimination
소매치기와 테러 발생	pickpocketing and terrorist incidences
관광객들에게 바가지요금을 씌우다	overcharge(rip off) tourists
여행객들에게 위험을 가하다	pose a risk(pose a threat/pose a danger) to tourists/threaten tourists
모험적인 활동에 참여하다/관련되다	get involved in(engage in) adventurous activities
위험한 활동에 의해 야기된	caused by(generated by/resulting from) risky activities
시차증에 걸리다	get jet lag/get time difference
언어장벽에 부딪치다	encounter(face/confront) language barriers(obstacles)
지역의 기준에 반하는	contrary to local norms
~로 보고된다	it is reported that S+V
이러한 이유들 때문에	on account of(because of/owing to/due to) those issues
그들이 처음 생각했던 것처럼 편안하지 않을지도 모른다	may not be relaxing as they first thought

CONCLUSION

결론은	In conclusion/to conclude/to sum up
모든 것을 고려할 때	all things considered/taking all things account(consideration)
분명하다	it is clear-cut(certain/obvious/clear/apparent) that S+V
귀중한	valuable/of value/worthwhile/precious
권장할 만한/바람직한	recommendable/reasonable/advisable/compelling/persuasive
훨씬 더 ~할 것 같다	be far(much) more likely to~

A가 B보다 중대하다/우세하다	A outweigh B
생명을 위협하는 활동들	life-threatening activities
안전을 최우선으로 하다	put safety as a priority

SENTENCE PRACTICE

INTRODUCTION

1. 최근에 저렴한 교통의 발달과 높은 생활 수준으로 외국으로 여행을 가는 사례들이 늘고 있다.

_____

_____

2. 외국을 여행하는 것이 여행객들에게 다른 나라의 문화와 역사를 경험하는 것을 가능하게 하는 것은 사실이다.

_____

_____

3. 그러나 여행을 할 때, 그들은 많은 어려움들을 겪는다.

_____

_____

4. 이 에세이에서, 나는 여행을 위해 외국에 가는 것에 대한 장단점들을 제시하겠다.

_____

_____

BODY 1

1. 다른 나라로 여행하는 것이 장점들을 가지고 있다는 것은 부인할 수 없다.

_____

_____

2. 첫 번째로, 해외여행을 하는 것은 방문한 나라의 문화, 사회과학 그리고 역사에 관해 다양한 경험을 제공할 것이다.

_____

_____

3. 여행객들은 많은 새로운 생각들과 많은 지식들과 접할 수 있기 때문에 이러한 유익한 경험들은 그들의 시야를 넓힐 수 있다.

_____

_____

4. 두 번째로, 특히 젊은 사람들은, 여행을 통해서 자립을 배울 수 있다.

_____

_____

5. 그들이 그들의 가족과 떨어져 있고 특히 혼자일 때, 그들은 때때로 예상하지 못한 상황이나 비상상황에 직면할 것이다.

_____

_____

6. 그러한 상황에서, 그들은 스스로 결정하고 문제들을 해결해야만 한다.

_____

_____

7. 따라서 여행은 세계에 대한 다양한 경험을 통해 시각을 넓히고 자립심을 기른다.

_____

_____

BODY 2

1. 다른 한편으로는 마찬가지로 해외여행에 대한 단점들이 있다.

_____

_____

2. 우선, 다른 나라를 방문하는 데 교통비, 숙박비를 포함한 상당히 많은 돈을 지불해야만 한다.

_____

_____

3. 그러므로, 사람들은 여행을 위해서 충분한 예산과 충분한 소득이 필요하다.

_____

_____

4. 이것뿐만 아니라, 여행하는 동안 산행, 스쿠버 다이빙 그리고 다른 위험한 활동들이 있다.

_____

_____

5. 이러한 것은 여행객들에게 위험을 가할 수 있다.

_____

_____

6. 만약 그러한 종류의 활동들로 인해 상해를 당한다면, 여행자들은 언어장벽과 다른 의료체계 때문에 치료하는 데 어려움에 직면할 수 있다.

_____

_____

7. 실제로 위험한 활동으로 인한 사고뿐만 아니라, 소매치기 그리고 최근 해외여행지에서의 테러와 같은 많은 사건들이 발생하고 있다.

_____

_____

8. 많은 사람들이 동유럽을 여행하는 동안 소지품들을 절도 당한 경험을 했다고 보도된다.

_____

_____

9. 이러한 문제들 때문에, 다른 나라를 여행하는 것은 처음 생각했던 것처럼 편안하지 않을지도 모른다.

_____

_____

CONCLUSION

1. 결론적으로 많은 요인들을 고려할 때, 비록 해외여행을 가는 것은 몇몇의 단점들이 있지만,

_____

_____

2. 여행자들이 해외여행을 통해 가치 있는 경험들과 기회들을 가질 수 있는 것은 분명하다.

_____

_____

3. 그러므로, 사람들이 다른 나라들을 여행하는 것은 권장할 만하다. 그러나 그들은 생명을 위협하는 활동들을 피해야만 하고 항상 안전을 최우선으로 둬야 한다.

_____

_____

ANSWER

INTRODUCTION

1. In recent years, the instances of traveling abroad have been on the rise with the development of cheaper transportation and a higher standard of living.

2. It is true that traveling overseas enables travelers to experience the culture and history of other nations.

3. Nevertheless, they go through many difficulties when taking a trip.

4. In this essay, I will present the pros and cons of going overseas for a trip.

BODY 1

1. It is undeniable that traveling to other countries has advantages.

2. Firstly, traveling abroad would provide a broad range of experiences regarding the culture, social sciences and history of the country people visit.

3. These enlightening experiences could broaden their horizons as they come across many novel ideas and much knowledge.

4. Secondly, travelers, especially young people, could learn independence through traveling.

5. When they are away from their family, particularly being alone, they will, at times, face unforeseen circumstances or emergencies.

6. In those situations, they would have to make decisions and solve problems by themselves.

7. Thus, traveling overseas widens the perspective of the world through a variety of experiences and cultivates self-reliance.

BODY 2

1. On the contrary, there are likewise the disadvantages of foreign trips.

2. For one, people have to spend a considerable amount of money on visiting other countries, including transportation, accommodation, and so on.

3. Hence, people need to have a big enough budget or sufficient income to travel.

4. Not only that, but there are also some activities such as mountain climbing, scuba diving, and other dangerous activities during traveling

5. , which can pose some risks to tourists.

6. If injured due to those kinds of activities, travelers could face difficulties in the treatment because of language barriers and the different medical system.

7. In fact, as well as accidents caused by risky activities, some incidents occurs like pickpocketing and the recent terrorist incidences in foreign tourist destinations.

8. It is reported that many people experienced having their belongings stolen while traveling around Eastern Europe.

9. On account of these issues, traveling to other countries may not be relaxing as they first thought.

CONCLUSION

1. In conclusion, considering many factors, though there are several drawbacks of traveling abroad.

2. It is clear-cut that tourists could have valuable experiences and opportunities through oversea traveling.

3. Hence, it is recommendable for people to travel to other countries, but they should avoid life-threatening activities and always put safety as a priority.

PREVIOUS TEST

1. People who travel to other countries should follow the customs and traditions of the country. To what extent do you agree or disagree? (2018.02.)

2. Some people believe that to protect local culture, tourism should be banned in some areas, whereas others think that changes are inevitable and banning tourism will have no benefits. Discuss both sides and give your opinion.

3. As a result of tourism, many historical buildings and sites are being damaged beyond repair. What could be done to prevent this?

** 첨삭은 **ieltseasywriting.com**

To address traffic problems, governments should tax private car owners heavily and use the money to improve public transportation. To what extent do you agree?

ESSENTIAL VOCA

INTRODUCTION

대중교통	public transportation/public transport
차량의 수	the number of cars(vehicles)
도로 교통량	the amount of road traffic
교통 혼잡	traffic congestion(jam)/bumper-to-bumper traffic/traffic gridlock
더욱 심각해지다	become more severe(serious/grave)
교통의 발달	the development of transportation
인구의 증가	population growth(explosion)/an increase in population
세금 정책	tax policy
과중한 세금	heavy(oppressive) taxes
~에 무거운 세금을 부과하다	impose(charge/levy/put/lay) heavy taxes on~
양날의 칼	a double-edged sword
장단점들	positive and negative points/advantages and disadvantages/pros and cons
실행 가능한 해결책들	feasible(possible/workable/actable/practicable/viable) solutions
개선하다	improve/develop/better
자세히 설명하다	elaborate on/spell out/explain in full detail

Unit
5
Culture

BODY 1(agree)

우선	to begin with/first and foremost/first of all
몇 가지 이점	a couple of(a few/several) benefits
잠재적인 차 구매자들	a potential(prospective) car buyer
A가 B 하는 것을 막다	discourage(deter/stop/prohibit) A from B
차 소유주들에게 부담이 되다	give(impose/lay) a burden to(on) car owners
개인용 차량 대신에	in place of(instead of/in lieu of) using private vehicles
대중교통을 이용하다	make use of(use/utilize/take) public transport/travel by public transportation
편안하고 편리한	comfortable and convenient
상태가 좋지 않다	be in an unfavorable condition
대중교통에 투자하다	invest in public transport/make an investment in public transportation
잘 정비된(설계된) 교통 시스템	a well-organized(a well-designed) transport system
운송 수단들	modes of transportation
교통 기반 시설	transport infrastructure
지하철	underground/subway/metro/tube
통근하다	commute to work
출퇴근 시간의 교통 혼잡	rush hour traffic
도로 통행료 징수	road pricing
과밀도로	an overcrowded road
교통 혼잡에 갇히다	be stuck in traffic/be in a traffic jam
교통체증을 차단하다	screen out traffic jam(congestion)/block traffic congestion(jam)
교통 혼잡 부담금	congestion charge(pricing)
A를 설득하여 B 하게 하다	persuade A into B(convince A of B)
교통문제를 줄이다	reduce(lessen/cut down on/alleviate) traffic problems
교통에 큰 영향(변화)을 주다	make a big difference to traffic
손상되기 쉬운/취약한 교통 환경	a fragile(damageable/vulnerable) traffic environment
A를 B 탓으로 돌리다	attribute(ascribe) A to B
A가 책임이 있다	A have(take) responsibility for/A be responsible(accountable) for/A be to blame for

차 소유주에게 세금을 부과하다	put(charge/levy) taxes on car owners
예를 들어	for example/for instance/for one thing
결과적으로/따라서	consequently/as a result/therefore/thus/hence/in this context

BODY 2(disagree)

반면에	on the flip side/on the other hand/on the contrary/in contrast
단점들	drawbacks/disadvantages/bad points/weaknesses
재정적 부담	a financial strain(burden/pressure)
특히	in particular/particularly/especially
이외에도	besides/aside from/other than
효과가 없다	go nowhere/be ineffective/have no effect at all/be unsuccessful
부자들	the haves/the wealthy/the affluent/the privileged
부가적인 세금을 낼 여력이 있다	can afford to pay additional taxes/be capable of pay additional taxes
A가 B 하도록 유도하다	lead(induce/drive) A to B
법에 따라	in compliance with the law/according to the law
교통 법규를 강화해야 한다	strengthen(beef up/intensify/reinforce) the traffic rules
교통법규를 지키다	obey(keep/follow/abide by) traffic rules
교통 법규를 어기다	violate(break/infringe/go against) traffic laws
~을 조심하다	take precautions against/be careful of/take a care of~
보행자 전용구역	pedestrian precinct/pedestrian-only area/road for pedestrian's exclusive use
부주의하고 공격적인 운전자들	a reckless and aggressive driver
제한 속도	speed limit/traffic speed
자동차 충돌 사고	a car crash/a rear-end collision
음주운전을 하다	drink-driving/drive under the influence of alcohol
음주운전과 과속	drinking violation and speeding
보행자들에게 위협을 가하다	pose a risk to(pose a threat to/threaten) pedestrians(walkers)
A를 B로부터 멀리하다	keep A away from B/keep A off B/A abstain from B

~와 관련이 있다	be linked to(be associated with/be related to)~
개선하는 데 중요한 역할을 하다	play a crucial(vital/critical) role in improving

CONCLUSION

결론은	in conclusion/to conclude/to sum up
위에서 언급한 것처럼	as stated above/as mentioned above
현재의 교통상황을 고려해 볼 때	given the current traffic situation
정책을 실시하다	implement(carry out/execute/enforce) a policy
가치가 있는	worthwhile/of value/valuable/meaningful
바람직한 해법	a recommendable(reasonable/advisable/desirable) solution
교통문제를 완화하다	ease(alleviate/relieve/relax/lighten) a traffic problem(concern/trouble)
~와 협력하다	team up with/cooperate with/work together with/go hand in hand with/collaborate with

SENTENCE PRACTICE

INTRODUCTION

1. 세계 전역의 도시들에서의 교통혼잡은 더욱 심각해지고 있다.

_____

_____

2. 이 문제에 대한 가능한 해결책은 개인 차량 운전자에게 과중한 세금을 부과하고 그 예산을 대중교통을 개선하는 데 사용하는 것이다.

_____

_____

3. 이 에세이는 이러한 정책의 장단점에 대해 자세히 설명할 것이다.

_____

_____

BODY 1

1. 우선, 더 나은 교통을 위해 차 소유주에게 세금을 부과하는 것은 몇 가지 이점이 있다.

_____

_____

2. 이점 중 하나는 과중한 세금은 잠재적인 차 구매자들이 차 구입하는 것을 주저하게 만들 것이라는 점이다.

_____

_____

3. 왜냐하면, 세금은 차 소유주들에게 부담을 주기 때문이다.

_____

_____

4. 개인용 차량을 이용하는 대신에, 그들은 대중교통을 이용할 것이고 이것은 교통문제를 줄일 것이다.

_____

_____

5. 다른 이점은, 세금은 대중교통을 더 편리하고 편안하게 만드는 데 사용될 수 있다.

_____

_____

6. 사실상, 많은 도시들이 대중교통 상태가 좋지 않다. 노후화된 버스들과 기차들은 덜 편안해서, 그런 이유로 사람들은 대중교통을 이용하지 않는다.

_____

_____

7. 만약 정부가 이러한 차량들을 개선하는 데 투자하면, 훨씬 더 많은 시민들이 그것을 이용할 것이고 교통 문제도 해결될 것이다.

_____

_____

8. 이것에 대한 한 가지 좋은 예로 싱가포르가 이 정책을 시행하는 첫 번째 나라들 중 하나이다.

_____

_____

9. 그리고 현재 그들은 잘 갖춰진 대중교통 시스템을 가지고 있다.

_____

_____

10. 이러한 맥락에서, 차 소유주에 대한 세금 부과는 실제로 교통문제를 줄일 수 있다.

_____

_____

BODY 2

1. 반면에, 이 해법에 대한 단점들이 있다.

_____

_____

2. 무엇보다 먼저, 차에 대한 높은 세금은 현재의 차 소유주들이나 운전자들에게 실질적인 부담이 될 것이다.

_____

_____

3. 특히, 사업을 위해서 차량이 필요한 사업자들은 재정적으로 심한 압박 상태에 놓일 수 있다.

_____

_____

4. 덧붙여서, 이러한 정책은 부자들에게 대중교통 이용을 유도하지 않기 때문에 효과적이지 않다.

_____

_____

5. 이것은 그들은 부가적인 세금을 내고 그들의 차를 살 여력이 있기 때문이다.

_____

_____

6. 그러므로, 운전자에게 세금을 부과하는 것은 교통문제를 해결하는 데 적절한 방법이 아니다.

_____

_____

CONCLUSION

1. 결론적으로, 이러한 정책을 시행하는 데는 장점들과 단점들이 있다.

_____

_____

2. 그러나, 현재의 교통 상황을 고려해 볼 때, 비록 몇 가지 단점들이 있지만, 나는 차 소유주들에게 세금을 부과하는 것은 가치가 있다는 것에 동의한다.

_____

_____

Unit

5

Culture

ANSWER

INTRODUCTION

1. Traffic congestion in cities around the world is becoming more severe.

2. One feasible solution to this problem is to impose heavy taxes on private car owners and use the budget to improve public transport.

3. This essay will spell out the positive and negative points of such a measure.

BODY 1

1. First of all, taxing on car owners for better traffic has a couple of benefits.

2. One of the advantages is that the heavy taxes would discourage prospective car buyers from purchasing cars

3. because taxes can give a burden to car owners.

4. In place of using private vehicles, they would begin to make use of public transport, which can also reduce traffic problems.

5. Another benefit is that the tax money could be used to make public transportation more convenient and comfortable.

6. In reality, public transport in many cities is in an unfavorable condition, old buses and trains are less comfortable, and this is one reason why most people do not use them.

7. If the government invests in the improvement of these vehicles, more citizens will use them, and traffic concerns will be unraveled.

8. An excellent example of this is Singapore which is one of the first countries to implement this policy.

9. And at present, they have a well-organized transport system.

10. In this context, putting taxes on car owners could indeed lessen traffic problems.

BODY 2

1. On the flip side, there are drawbacks to this solution.

2. First and foremost, high taxes on cars would be put a real financial strain on current car owners and drivers.

3. In particular, business people who need vehicles for business could be under heavier financial pressure.

4. Besides, this policy goes nowhere since this type of tax will not lead the haves to use public transportation.

5. This is because they can afford to buy their cars and pay additional taxes.

6. Therefore, levying taxes on car owners is not the proper way to tackle traffic concerns.

CONCLUSION

1. In conclusion, there are the merit and demerits of introducing such a policy.

2. However, given the current traffic situation, I agree that charging taxes on car owners, although having a few weaknesses, is worthwhile.

PREVIOUS TEST

---

1. Most people believe that stricter punishment should be given for traffic offenses. To what extent do you agree? (2018.)

2. Some people think that to solve traffic and transportation problems, people should be encouraged to live in cities rather than in the suburbs in the countryside. To what extent do you agree or disagree?

3. One way to solve the problem of congestion on the roads is to increase the tax on private vehicles. How could this alleviate congestion?
How other measures can you suggest to deal with congestion in cities?

** 첨삭은 **ieltseasywriting.com**

Health

1. Health and diet

2. Obesity

3. Smoking

1. Health and diet

Some people believe that it is the responsibility of individuals to take care of their own health and diet. Others, however, believe that governments should make sure that their citizens have a healthy diet. What is your opinion?

ESSENTIAL VOCA

INTRODUCTION

건강과 식단	health and diet
증가하는 많은 사람들	an increasing(rising/growing) number of people
건강 문제를 겪다	suffer from(struggle with/go through) a health concern(problem/trouble)
계속되어 온 문제가 되다	become an ongoing(continual/lasting) issue
정신적, 육체적 건강	mental and physical health
삶의 질	the quality of life
평균기대수명	average life expectancy(span)
건강을 유지하다	keep fit/keep in shape/get in shape
반면에	while/whereas/whilst/on the other hand
A가 책임이 있다	A be responsible(accountable) for/A have(shoulder/take) the responsibility for
~에 좌우하다/달려있다	be up to/depend on/rely on/have a dependency on~
제시하다	present/show/propose/suggest
~에 대해 자세히 설명하다	elaborate on/explain in detail/spell out

BODY 1(individuals)

우선	to begin with/first of all/in the first place/first and foremost
건강과 관련해서	concerning(regarding/as regards/with respect to/in relation to) health
개인적 차원에서	on a personal level(side)
자유의지	free will/free volition
~을 돌보다	look after/take care of/care for~
연 1회 건강 검진	annual check-up
운동하다	work out/exercise/take exercise/do exercise
실내외 운동	indoor and outdoor exercise
선택하다	make a choice/choose/select
어떤 종류의 음식	what sorts(kinds/types) of food
균형 잡힌 식단	a well-balanced diet
빈약한 식단	a poor(unhealthy) diet/an unbalanced diet
불규칙한 식습관	an irregular eating pattern(habit)
과식	overeating/excessive eating
생활 방식	the way of life
좌식 생활 방식	the sedentary lifestyle
혹독한 식단관리를 하다	go on a strict diet
칼로리를 줄이다	reduce(lessen/cut down on/cut back on/alleviate) calories
음식에 대한 지나친 욕구를 억제하다	curb(suppress/control/stop) a food craving(a craving for food)
아이들 건강에 대해 말하자면	in the case of(when it comes to/in terms of) children's health
부모의 의무이고 책임	parents' obligation and responsibility
A에게 B 하지 않도록 지도하다(권장하다)	guide A not to B/encourage A not to B
개인의 책임이다	be down to individuals
~에 해로운 영향을 주다	Have(exert) a harmful(detrimental/pernicious/adverse/negative) influence(impact/effect) on

BODY 2(governments)

그럼에도 불구하고	nevertheless/for all that/nonetheless/still
사실상	in fact/in reality/actually/virtually/as a matter of fact
~하지 않을 수 없다	have little choice but to+V/cannot but+V/cannot help ~ing
바쁜 생활양식 때문에	on account of(due to/because of/owing to) a very hectic(busy) lifestyle
질 낮은 음식	low-quality food
준비하기 쉬운 음식	easy-to-prepare food/convenience food
외식의 편리함	convenience of eating out
포장음식	packed food/take away food
미리 만든 음식	ready-made food
칼로리가 높다(낮다)	be high(low) in calories
포화(불포화)지방이 많다(적다)	be rich(low) in high saturated(unsaturated) fat
의료혜택	a health benefit/a health care benefit
좋은 건강관리 제도	the good health care system
의무적 건강보험	compulsory health insurance
~에 대한 규정을 만들다	make regulations about~
시행하다/실시하다	implement/enforce/put in force/practice/carry out/conduct
법규에 대한 적절한 실행을 위해	for the proper implementation of rules
그 일을 위임받은	entrusted with the job
특별한 부서를 설립하다	set up(establish/found) a particular department
음식 재료/성분들	ingredients/food sources
패스트푸드를 제한하다	restrict(control/curb/stop/prohibit) fast food
패스트푸드에 세금을 부과하다	impose(levy/charge) taxes on fast food
강한 예방 조치를 하다	take strong precautions
심리적 치료	psychological treatment
개입 프로그램을 만들다	set up(establish) an intervention program
개선하다	improve/enhance/better
보건복지부	the Ministry of Health and Welfare

건강과 관련된 캠페인	campaigns concerning health/a health-related campaign
공익광고	public service announcement
좋은 건강의 중요성을 알다	be aware of the importance of good health
조기 사망 위험성을 낮추다	lower the risk of premature(untimely) death
운동 시설을 설치하다	set up(install/build/equip) sports facilities
운동 시설에 접근하다	have access to(access/get access to) health and fitness facilities
운동할 기회를 갖다	have an opportunity(chance/occasion) to work out
정신과 건강을 풍요롭게 하다	enrich mind and health
A에게 B를 권장하다	encourage A to B
A가 B 하는 것을 못 하게 하다	discourage A from B
도움이 되다	be of help(benefit)/be helpful(beneficial)
상당한 영향을 주다	have a great(considerable/significant) effect(influence/impact) on
해결하다	address/tackle/battle/settle/sort out/solve
이처럼/이와 같이	like this/in this way/in this regard/in this manner
따라서/그러므로	thus/therefore/as a result/consequently/in this context/hence

CONCLUSION

요약하자면	to sum up/in conclusion/to conclude/in short
A를 고려하다	take A into consideration(account)/consider A
해야만 한다	ought to/should/had better/be supposed to
일반 대중	the public/the general public
건강에 중요한 역할을 하다	play a crucial(vital/important/significant/essential) role in health
이치에 맞다	make sense/stand to reason/be logical
조치를 취하다	take measures(steps/action)
~와 협력하다	team up with/cooperate with/work together with/go hand in hand with
핵심은 ~이다	the bottom line is that S+V

SENTENCE PRACTICE

INTRODUCTION

1. 점점 더 많은 사람들이 건강문제들을 겪고 있다.

_____

_____

2. 그 결과, 건강과 식단은 많은 국가에서 계속된 문제가 되고 있다.

_____

_____

3. 어떤 사람들은 국민의 건강을 개선시키는 데 국가가 책임을 져야 한다고 주장한다.

_____

_____

4. 반면에, 다른 사람들은 그것은 개인에 달려 있다고 말한다.

_____

_____

5. 이 에세이는 이 논쟁의 두 가지 측면을 자세히 설명하겠다,

_____

_____

BODY 1

1. 우선 개개인이 그들의 다이어트와 건강에 책임감을 가져야만 한다.

_____

_____

2. 성인들은 자유의지를 가지고 있고 그들이 할 운동과 어떤 종류의 음식을 먹을 건지 스스로 선택한다.

_____

_____

3. 이런 의미에서, 다이어트와 건강을 돌보는 것은 개인의 태도에 달려 있다.

_____

_____

4. 덧붙여서, 어린이 건강에 대해 말하자면, 그것은 부모의 의무와 책임이다.

_____

_____

5. 그것은 그들이 균형 잡힌 식단을 주어야 하고 햄버거, 프라이드 치킨 그리고 인스턴트 누들과 같은 정크푸드를 먹지 않도록 지도해야 하기 때문이다.

_____

_____

6. 그러므로, 건강과 식단은 정부가 아니라 개개인의 책임이다.

_____

_____

BODY 2

1. 그러나, 정부에 대해서 말하자면, 그들은 또한 사람들의 건강과 다이어트에 책임이 있다.

_____

_____

2. 현대사회에서 사람들은 집에서나 직장에서의 바쁜 생활 때문에 설탕, 소금 그리고 지방이 높은 패스트푸드 또는 미리 준비된 음식에 의존하지 않을 수 없다.

_____

_____

3. 정부가 건강 문제를 해결하기 위해서, 그들은 판매하는 음식에 사용되는 음식 재료에 대한 일정한 규정을 만들어야 한다.

_____

_____

4. 법규에 대한 적절한 실행을 위해서 그 일을 위임받은 특별한 부서를 설립함과 함께 정부의 개입이 있어야 한다.

_____

_____

5. 더욱이 정부는 건강과 건강한 다이어트에 대한 캠페인과 같은 예방 조치에 많은 예산을 사용해야 한다.

_____

_____

6. 예를 들어, 우리나라가 실행하는 건강 캠페인들 중 하나로서, 보건복지부에 의한 건강에 대한 TV 공익광고들이 있다.

_____

_____

7. 그것은 일반 대중들에게 건강을 유지하는 것에 대한 중요성을 알게 하는 데 도움이 되고 있다.

_____

_____

8. 이러한 맥락에서, 정부가 사람들의 건강과 건강한 음식의 장려에 책임을 가져야 하는 것은 분명하다.

_____

_____

CONCLUSION

1. 요약하자면, 이 주제의 두 가지 측면을 고려할 때, 개인들이 그들의 건강과 식단을 돌봐야 한다.

_____

_____

2. 정부는 시민들을 위한 건강과 식단에 있어 훨씬 더 중요한 역할을 해야만 한다.

_____

_____

3. 따라서, 핵심은 정부와 개개인들은 건강과 식단을 개선하기 위해 서로 협력해야만 한다는 것이다.

_____

_____

ANSWER

INTRODUCTION

1. An increasing number of people are suffering from health problems.

2. As a result, health and diet become an ongoing issue in many countries.

3. Some people argue that governments should be responsible for improving people's health

4. , while others say that it is up to individuals.

5. This essay will elaborate on both sides of the argument.

BODY 1

1. To begin with, individuals should have the responsibility for their diet and health.

2. Adults have their free will and make their choice about what sorts of food they eat and the exercise they do.

3. In this sense, caring for diet and health has a dependency on an individual's attitude.

4. On top of that, in the case of children's health, it is the parents' obligation and responsibility.

5. It is because they should give a well-balanced diet and guide their children not to eat junk food such as hamburgers, fried chicken, and instant noodles.

6. Health and diet are, therefore, down to individuals, not governments.

BODY 2

1. However, when it comes to states, they are accountable for people's health and diet as well.

2. People in modern society have little choice but to depend on fast food or ready-made meals, which are high in sugar, salt and fat on account of a very hectic lifestyle at home and in the workplace.

3. For governments to address health concern, they should make regulations about ingredients used in selling foods.

4. There should be governmental intervention, with setting up a particular department entrusted with the job, for the proper implementation of rules.

5. Furthermore, governments should spend massive amounts of tax funds on preventative measures such as campaigns concerning health and healthy diet.

6. For instance, as one health campaign that our country has implemented, there are public service announcements on TV for good health by The Ministry of Health Welfare.

7. This is of help to make the general public aware of the importance of keeping fit.

8. In this context, it is clear-cut that governments should shoulder the responsibility for people's health and encouragement of healthy food.

CONCLUSION

1. To sum up, taking both sides of the issue into account, individuals ought to look after their health and food.

2. Governments should play a much more crucial role in the health and diet of the citizens.

3. Thus, the bottom line is that governments and individuals should team up with each other to improve health and diet.

PREVIOUS TEST

1. In many countries, the tradition of families having meals together is disappearing. Why is this happening? What will be the effects of it on the family and society? (2018.)

2. With a fast pace of modern life, more and more people are turning towards fast food for their main meals.
Do you think the advantages outweigh the disadvantages?

3. With a growing population, many people believe that we should focus on producing more GM foods. What are the advantages and disadvantages of doing this?

** 첨삭은 ieltseasywriting.com

2. Obesity

The issue of obesity is a growing concern around the world. It affects children as well as adults. What are the reasons for this rise in obesity? How can it be tackled?

ESSENTIAL VOCA

INTRODUCTION

비만	obesity/overweight
계속된 문제	an ongoing(continual/lasting) issue
증가하는 비만의 비율	a rising(an increasing) rate of obesity
건강문제	health concerns(problems/troubles)
질병에 걸리다	develop(come down with/contract) a disease
뇌졸중/당뇨/심장질환	a stroke/diabetes/heart disease
원인	a cause(culprit/reason/factor/source)
전자/후자	the former(the one)/the latter(the other)
~에 상당한 영향을 끼치다	have(exert) great(considerable/significant/broad) effects(influences) on~
이외에도/덧붙여서	besides/furthermore/in addition/additionally
A뿐만 아니라 B	not only A but also B/B as well as A
실행 가능한 방법들	possible(workable/feasible/practicable/viable) ways
해결하다	address/tackle/battle/settle/sort out/unravel
제시하다	present/show/propose/suggest
~에 대해 자세히 설명하다	elaborate on/explain in detail/spell out

BODY 1(causes)

우선	to begin with/first of all/in the first place/first and foremost
비만 원인과 관련해서	concerning(regarding/as regards/with respect to/in relation to) the causes of obesity
빈약한 식단	a poor(unhealthy) diet
보통 사람들	ordinary(average/normal) people
반복되는 일상	daily routines
좌식 생활 방식	a sedentary lifestyle
바쁜 사회에서	in an on-the-go society
바쁘게 살다	lead(live) a busy life
불규칙한 식습관	an irregular eating pattern
제대로 된 식사 준비할 시간이 없다	have little time to prepare for decent meals
~에 해로운 영향을 주다	Have(has) harmful(detrimental/pernicious/adverse/negative) influences(impacts/effects) on
몸과 마음에 큰 타격을 주다	take a heavy toll on one's body and mind
육체적 정신적 건강을 위험에 처하게 하다	endanger(threaten) the physical and mental well-being
음식을 준비하는 부담	the burden of preparing for foods
칼로리가 높다	be high in calories
~에 좌우하다	be up to/depend on/rely on/have a dependency on~
건강하지 않은 재료들	unhealthy ingredients
식품 첨가물	food additives
방부제/조미료	preservative/artificial flavors
가공식품	processed food
포장음식	packed food/take away food
미리 만든 음식	ready-made food
접근성, 적절한 가격 그리고 편리함 때문에	because of accessibility, affordable prices and convenience
음식 재료/성분들	ingredients/food sources
식욕	appetite
편식	an unbalanced diet
과식	overeating/excessive eating

부작용	a side effect/an adverse reaction
비만과 관련된 질병들	obesity-related diseases
살을 빼다/살이 찌다	lose weight/gain(get) weight
병을 악화시키다	aggravate(worsen) illness
합병증이 생기다	develop a complication/a complication arises
질병에 취약하다	be vulnerable(susceptible/sensitive) to illnesses
~에 알레르기가 있다	be allergic to+Ⓝ
건강에 독이 되다	be toxic to(be poisonous to) health
더 높은 사망 위험성	a higher risk of death
우울증	depression
식이장애	eating disorder
만성피로증후군	chronic fatigue syndrome
수면과 관련된 문제	a sleep-related problem
수면 장애	sleep disturbance(disorder)
수면 부족	a lack of sleep
불면증을 겪다	suffer from insomnia
면역체계에 손상을 주다	undermine(damage/compromise) immune system
만성적인 질병을 겪다	suffer from(go through) chronic diseases
생리적이고 심리적인 문제들	physiological and psychological problems
적절한 음식의 대한 지식의 부족	lack of knowledge of proper food
건강의 위험에 대한 무지	the unawareness of health risks
절제되지 않은 먹는 습관에 의해 야기된	caused by(generated by/resulting from) uncontrolled eating habits.
비만 때문에 괴롭힘을 경험하다	experience bullying due to obesity
자존감에 영향을 주다	affect self-esteem
비만을 야기하다	give rise to(lead to/result in/bring about) overweight(obesity)
비만에 상당히 기여하다	contribute a great deal to obesity/make a considerable contribution to obesity
~을 겪다/~로부터 고통받다	go through/suffer from/struggle with
칼로리를 소모하다	consume(burn) calories

~할 기회를 갖다	have(has) opportunities(chances/occasions) to~
위 원인의 결과로서	as the result of the above factors
이처럼/이와 같이	like this/in this way/in this manner/in this regard
따라서/그러므로	as a result/hence/consequently/in this context/therefore

BODY 2(solutions)

그럼에도 불구하고	nevertheless/in spite of that/for all that/nonetheless/still
~에 관해서는	in the case of/when it comes to/with respect to/in terms of
건강의 중요성을 알다	be aware of the importance of good health
균형 잡힌 식단	a well-balanced diet
패스트푸드에 세금을 부과하다	impose(levy/charge) taxes on fast food
그 제품을 싸게 만들지 않도록	in order not to make the products so cheap
개인적 차원에서	on a personal level/personally
운동하다	work out/exercise
운동 시설들	health and fitness facilities
접근하다	access/have(get/gain) access to)+Ⓝ
실내외 운동	indoor and outdoor exercise
운동 시설을 설치하다	set up(equip/build) sports facilities
치료를 받다	receive medical treatment
스트레스를 해소하다	relieve(release) stress
필수 영양소	essential nutrients
삶의 질/생활방식	the quality of life/the way of life
건강을 유지하다	keep fit/keep in shape/get in shape
정신과 건강을 풍요롭게 하다	enrich mind and health
건강을 돌보다	look after(take care of/care for) health
음식에 대한 지나친 욕구를 억제하다	curb(suppress/control/stop) food cravings
지방 흡수량을 줄이다	reduce(curtail/cut down on/cut back on) fat intake

제한하다	restrict/control/curb/stop/prohibit
혹독한 식단관리를 하다	go on a strict diet
포화지방이 많이 함유된	rich in high saturated fat
놀라운 영향	incredible(alarming/remarkable) impacts(influences/effects)
보건복지부	the Ministry of Health and Welfare
공익광고	public service announcement(advertisement)
예방조치	preventative measures(steps/action)
A에게 B를 하지 않도록 지도하다	guide A not to B/encourage A not to B
덧붙여서	on top of that/in addition to that/not only that
이런 의미에서	in this sense/in this way/in this manner
~하지 않도록	in order not to/so as not to
따라서/그러므로	thus/therefore/as a result/consequently/in this context

CONCLUSION

요약하자면	to sum up/in conclusion/to conclude/in short
상황들	circumstances/situation/conditions
조치들	measures/steps/action
비만을 극복하다	overcome(get over/cope with) obesity
~에 책임이 있다	be responsible(accountable) for/have(take) responsibility for/be to blame for
시행하다/실시하다	implement/enforce/put in force/practice/carry out/conduct
이치에 맞다	make sense/stand to reason/be logical
~와 협력하다	cooperate with/team up with/work together with/go hand in hand with
핵심은 ~이다	the bottom line is that S+V

Unit

6

Health

SENTENCE PRACTICE

INTRODUCTION

1. 비만은 우리가 현재 직면한 계속 진행 중인 건강 문제 중의 하나이다.

_____

_____

2. 비만인 사람들이 훨씬 더 당뇨병, 심장 질환 그리고 뇌졸중 같은 질병에 잘 걸릴 수 있다는 것은 사실이다.

_____

_____

3. 이외에도, 비만은 성인 건강뿐만 아니라 아이들 성장에도 상당한 영향을 준다.

_____

_____

4. 이 에세이에서, 나는 비만을 해결하기 위한 원인들과 가능한 방법들을 제시하겠다.

_____

_____

BODY 1

1. 우선, 이 문제에 대한 주요한 원인은 빈약한 식단이다.

_____

_____

2. 오늘날, 사람들은 항상 바쁘고 제대로 된 식사를 준비할 시간이 거의 없다.

_____

_____

3. 대부분의 사람들은 그들의 바쁜 생활 방식 때문에 종종 칼로리가 높고, 중독성 그리고 보존력이 있는 포장음식들과 미리 만든 음식을 종종 선택한다.

_____

_____

4. 사실상, 지난 10년에 걸쳐서 패스트푸드 레스토랑의 수는 상당한 증가를 해왔고 패스트푸드는 삶의 방식이 되어 오고 있다. 이것은 사람들이 비만이 되게 한다.

_____

_____

5. 비만을 상당히 일으키는 다른 요인들은 대부분 사람들이 갖는 좌식 생활 양식이다.

_____

_____

6. 일반적으로, 많은 사람들은 요즘 직장에서 그리고 집에서 오랫동안 컴퓨터 앞에 앉는다.

_____

_____

7. 따라서, 그들은 그들이 섭취하는 칼로리를 소모시키는 기회를 가질 수 없고, 그것은 그들의 급격한 체중 증가로 이어진다.

_____

_____

BODY 2

1. 그럼에도 불구하고, 비만 문제를 해결하는 몇 가지 방법들이 있다.

_____

_____

2. 정부에 관해서는, 그들은 좋은 건강의 중요성을 소비자들에게 알림으로써 패스트푸드와 포장된 음식을 먹지 못하도록 할 수 있다.

_____

_____

3. 덧붙여서, 정부는 그 상품들을 구매하기 쉬운 것으로 만들지 않게 하기 위해서 그들에게 세금을 부과해야 한다.

_____

_____

4. 지역 공동체에 관해서는 그들은 또한 시민들이 쉽게 접근할 수 있는 지역 사회 센터에 체육관을 지음으로써 운동하도록 권장해야 한다.

_____

_____

5. 한 예로써, 일부의 지역 센터의 경우에, 당국은 시민들을 위해 다양한 운동 시설들을 갖춘 지역 체육관이나 공원을 설치해 오고 있다.

_____

_____

6. 그들은 효율적으로 운영되고 있고 지역 시민들에 의해 환영받고 있다.

_____

_____

7. 개인적인 차원에서, 사람들은 정기적으로 운동하고 건강한 음식을 먹음으로써 그들의 건강을 돌보도록 노력해야 한다.

_____

_____

8. 이와 같이 비만을 피하기 위한 실행 가능한 해결책들이 있다.

_____

_____

CONCLUSION

1. 요약하자면, 몇몇의 상황들은 비만을 일으킨다. 그러나, 또한 비만을 극복하기 위한 몇 가지 조치들이 있다.

_____

_____

2. 이것과 관련해서, 정부와 공동체들은 비만 문제를 해결하기 위해서 시민들과 협력해야 한다.

_____

_____

ANSWER

INTRODUCTION

1. Obesity is one of the ongoing health concerns we face today.

2. In is a fact that obese people are far more likely to develop diseases such as diabetes, health problems, and strokes.

3. Besides, obesity has considerable impacts on not only adult health but also children's growth.

4. In this essay, I will present causes and possible ways to sort out overweight.

BODY 1

1. To begin with, the primary source of this problem is a poor diet.

2. Today, people are always in a great hurry and have little time to prepare decent meals.

3. Most people, due to their hectic lifestyles, often choose packaged foods and ready-made meals which are high in calories, additives, and preservatives.

4. In fact, over the last decade, there has been a significant increase in the number of fast food restaurants, and fast food has become a way of life, which gives rise to people being overweight.

5. Another factor that contributes a great deal to obesity is a sedentary lifestyle most people have.

6. In general, plenty of people nowadays sit in front of the computer for a long time at their workplace and home.

7. As a result, they cannot have any opportunities to consume the calories they take, which lead to their rapid gaining of weight.

BODY 2

1. Nevertheless, there are several methods to address the obesity problem.

2. In the case of governments, they can discourage people from eating fast food and packaged foods by getting consumers to be aware of the importance of good health.

3. Moreover, governments should impose heavier taxes on them in order not to make the products so cheap.

4. When it comes to communities, they should also encourage citizens to work out by building gyms in community centers that citizens can have easy access to.

5. For one thing. concerning some community center, the authorities have equipped local gyms and parks with various health and fitness facilities for their citizens.

6. They have been operated efficiently and hailed by local citizens.

7. On a personal level, individuals should try to look after their health by eating healthy foods and exercising regularly.

8. Like this, there are viable solutions to avoid obesity.

CONCLUSION

1. To sum up, several circumstances result in obesity. However, there are also a few measures that be taken to overcome obesity.

2. In this context, governments and communities should cooperate with citizens to unravel obesity concerns.

PREVIOUS TEST

1. An increasing number of children are overweight which could result in many problems when they grow older both regarding their health and health care costs. Why do you think so many children are overweight? What could be done to solve this problem?

2. Over the last few decades,, the media has promoted the image of thin young women as being ideal. What problems has this caused?
What solutions can you suggest to this issue?

3. The amount of time spent on sport and exercise should be increased in schools in order to tackle the problem of overweight children?
Do you think this is the best way to deal with the problem?
What other solutions can you suggest?

** 첨삭은 ieltseasywriting.com

3. Smoking

In some countries, people are no longer allowed to smoke in many public places and office buildings. Do you think this is a good rule or a bad rule?

ESSENTIAL VOCA

INTRODUCTION

최근에	in recent years/in recent times/recently
금연 정책	an anti-smoking(smoking-free) policy
공공장소에서의 흡연에 대해	regarding(concerning/as regards) smoking in public places(areas)
대중의 이목/높은 관심	a high profile
건강 문제들	health concerns(problems/troubles)
주요한	leading/primary/major/main
그럼에도 불구하고	nevertheless/for all that/nonetheless/still
논쟁	an argument(issue/debate/controversy/discussion)
전자/후자	the former(the one)/the latter(the other)
상황들	circumstances/situations/conditions
실행 가능한 해법	a feasible(workable/viable/practicable) solution
금연 정책을 시행하다	implement(enforce/carry out/conduct) an anti-smoking(smoke-free) policy
제한되어야 한다	should be discouraged(restricted/prohibited)
다음은 이유들이다	the following are the reasons

BODY 1(healthy factors)

우선	to begin with/first of all/first and foremost/in the first place
건강에 대해 말하자면	when it comes to(in terms of/in the case of) health
간접흡연자	a second-hand smoker/a passive smoker
일반 대중	the public/the general public
담배를 많이 피우는 사람	a heavy-smoking person
~에 해로운 영향을 주다	have(exert) harmful(detrimental/pernicious/adverse/negative) influences(impacts/effects) on
A에 상당한 기여를 하다	contribute a great deal to A(make a considerable contribution to A/A be greatly attributed to)
연구에 따르면	according to research
보고되고 있다	it is reported that S+V
육체적 정신적 건강을 위험에 처하게 하다	endanger the physical and mental wellbeing
병을 악화시키다	aggravate(worsen) an illness
건강상 위험을 야기하다(초래하다)	result in(give rise to/lead to/bring about) health hazards
유해한 화학물질들	detrimental(harmful/injurious) chemicals
높은 사망 위험성	a higher risk of death
부작용	a side effect/an adverse reaction
치명적 질병	a fatal(deadly/lethal) disease
만성피로증후군	chronic fatigue syndrome
암, 천식 발작 그리고 폐질환 발병	the development of cancers, asthma attacks, and lung infections
수면 장애	sleep disturbances(disorders)
조기사망	a premature(an untimely) death
건강에 독이 되다	be toxic to(be poisonous to) health
질병에 걸리다	develop(contract/come down with) diseases
질병에 걸리기 쉽다(취약하다)	be susceptible(vulnerable/sensitive) to illness
담배와 관련된 질병으로 죽다	die from smoking-related diseases

BODY 2(educational factors)

교육에 대해서	as regards(regarding/concerning) education
청소년	adolescents/teenagers/schoolchildren
담배에 노출되다	be exposed to(get exposure to) smoking
미래에 흡연자가 되다	become a smoker in the future
흡연이 용인되다(받아들여지다)	smoking is acceptable
~하는 경향이 있다	tend to/have a tendency to/be inclined to/be liable to~
몸과 마음에 큰 타격을 주다	take a toll on one's body and mind
담배를 피우지 않는 생활태도	a tobacco-free lifestyle
증가하는 청소년 흡연을 막다	thwart the growing number of juvenile smoking

BODY 3(environmental aspects)

환경적인 관점에서	from an environmental standpoint(viewpoint/perspective)
환경적인 문제를 야기하다	cause(generate/create/trigger/provoke) environmental problems
많은 돈	a lot of(a good deal of/a high amount of/a considerable amount of) money
쓰레기	trash/waste/rubbish/garbage/litter
담배꽁초를 버리다	throw away(discard/abandon) cigarette butts(ends)
청소하다	clean up/sweep
집중호우	torrential(heavy) rains/localized heavy rains(downpour)
쌓이다/누적하다	accumulate/pile up
그 주변환경을 손상시키다	undermine(damage/compromise/impair/hurt) the surroundings
기본적인 인간의 권리를 위협하다	threaten fundamental human rights
담배 연기로부터 고통받다	go through(suffer from/struggle with) cigarette smoke
환경적 이유 때문에	due to(owing to/because of/on account of) environmental reasons
A가 B 하는 것을 못 하게 하다(권장하다)	discourage(encourage) A from B

CONCLUSION

요약하자면	to sum up/in conclusion/to conclude/in short
A를 고려하다	take A into consideration(account)/consider A
관련된 단체들	organizations involved
이치에 맞다	make sense/stand to reason/be logical
해야만 한다	ought to/should/had better/be supposed to
건강을 유지하다	keep fit/keep in shape/get in shape
대단히 도움이 되다	be of great help(be helpful/be of great benefit/be beneficial)
~에 대한 규정을 만들다	make regulations about~
법규에 대한 적절한 실행	the implement of rules
올바른 정책을 시행하다	implement(enforce/put in force/practice/carry out/conduct) the right policy
금연장소로 지정되다	be designated as smoke-free areas
흡연을 금지하다/억제하다	curb(stop/prohibit) smoking
~와 협력하다	cooperate with/team up with/work together with~
핵심은 ~이다	the bottom line is that S+V

SENTNECE PRACTICE

INTRODUCTION

1. 최근에 공공장소에서의 흡연에 대한 많은 논쟁들이 대중의 이목을 끌고 있다.

_____

_____

2. 영국과 같은 몇몇 국가들은 지금 공공장소에서 엄격한 흡연 금지 정책을 시행하고 있다.

_____

_____

3. 그럼에도 불구하고, 일부 사람들은 여전히 공공장소에서 담배를 피운다.

_____

_____

4. 나는 흡연이 공공장소에서 금지되어야 한다는 의견을 가지고 있다. 다음은 이유들이다.

_____

_____

BODY 1

1. 건강에 대해서 말하자면, 공공장소에서의 흡연은 흡연자들이나 비흡연자들에게 해로운 영향을 끼친다.

_____

_____

2. 담배가 암의 발생, 천식발작 그리고 폐질환에 상당히 원인이 되는 수많은 해로운 화학 물질을 포함하고 있다는 것은 사실이다.

_____

_____

3. 특히, 임산부와 어린이 같은 취약한 건강 문제를 가진 사람들은 간접흡연자들로서 더 심각하게 영향을 받을 수 있다.

_____

_____

4. 연구에 따르면, 한 사람이 흡연자이고 다른 사람이 비흡연자인 결혼한 커플일 경우,

_____

_____

5. 후자는 간접흡연 때문에 전자보다 30% 이상 높은 심장질환 사망률을 가지고 있다고 보고되고 있다.

_____

_____

6. 이러한 이유들 때문에, 공공장소에서 흡연은 금지되어야 한다.

_____

_____

BODY 2

1. 교육에 관련하여, 흡연환경에 노출된 어린이들은 미래에 흡연자가 될 가능성이 크다.

_____

_____

2. 그것은 그들은 흡연을 받아들일 수 있다고 생각하는 경향이 있기 때문이다.

_____

_____

3. 만약에 공공장소에서의 흡연이 허용되면, 어린이들은 흡연에 자연스럽게 노출될 것이고, 그것은 좋은 본보기가 되지 않는다.

_____

_____

4. 따라서, 공공장소는 아이들의 교육과 발달을 위해서 금연장소로 지정되어야 한다.

_____

_____

BODY 3

1. 환경적인 관점에서, 공공장소에서의 흡연은 또한 환경적 문제를 발생시킨다.

_____

_____

2. 한 가지 예로, 담배꽁초나 재가 쌓이면 그것은 집중 폭우로 국지적인 범람을 일으킬 수 있다.

_____

_____

3. 이것은 흡연자들이 흡연 후에 쓰레기를 아무데나 버리기 때문이다.

_____

_____

4. 사실상, 우리는 지하철 역이나 버스 정류장들 주변에서 흡연자들에 의해 버려진 쓰레기를 쉽게 볼 수 있다.

_____

_____

5. 이것은 주변 환경을 해치고 있으며, 청소하는 데 상당한 비용이 든다.

_____

_____

6. 따라서, 공공장소에서의 흡연은 환경적인 이유들 때문에 허용되어서는 안 된다.

_____

_____

CONCLUSION

1. 결론은, 모든 것을 고려할 때, 흡연이 공공장소에서 금지되어야 하는 몇 가지 이유들이 있다.

_____

_____

2. 따라서, 정부들과 관련된 당국들은 공공장소에서 흡연을 금지하기 위한 법규를 강화하는 것이 바람직하다.

_____

_____

Unit

6

Health

ANSWER

INTRODUCTION

1. In recent years, a lot of controversies regarding smoking in public places have been a high profile.

2. Several countries, like the UK, now implement a strict anti-smoking policy in public spaces.

3. Nevertheless, some people still smoke in public areas.

4. I am of the view that smoking should be discouraged in public places. The following are the reasons.

BODY 1

1. When it comes to health, smoking in public places has harmful effects on both smokers and non-smokers.

2. It is true that tobacco contains numerous detrimental chemicals which contribute a great deal to the development of cancers, asthma attacks , and lung infections

3. In particular, people with vulnerable health care concerns like pregnant women and children could be more severely affected as second-hand smokers.

4. According to research, in case of a married couple where one partner is a smoker and the other a non-smoker.

5. The latter is reported to have a 30 percent higher risk of death from heart disease than the former because of passive smoking.

6. For these reasons, smoking in public areas should be prohibited.

BODY 2

1. As regards education, children exposed to a smoking environment are more likely to become smokers in the future

2. , which is why they tend to think smoking is acceptable.

3. If smoking is allowed in public places, children will get exposure to smoking naturally, and it does not set a good example.

4. Thus, public places should be designated as smoke-free areas for children education.

BODY 3

1. From an environmental standpoint, smoking in public places also causes environmental problems.

2. For one thing, cigarette butts and ash are accumulated, which can result in localized overflowing after torrential rains.

3. It is because smokers in public throw away their waste anywhere after smoking.

4. In fact, we can easily see trash thrown by smokers all over subway stations and bus stops.

5. It undermines the surroundings and cost a lot of money to clean up.

6. Hence, smoking in public areas should not be permitted due to environmental reasons.

CONCLUSION

1. In conclusion, considering all those things, there are several reasons why smoking should be banned in public places.

2. Thus, it makes sense that governments and organizations involved should enforce the rules to curb smoking in public.

PREVIOUS TEST

1. Many people say smoking should be banned and some say it is not a good idea. What is your opinion on this?

2. Smoking can cause serious illness and should be made illegal. To what extent do you agree?

3. Tobacco is a kind of drug. People have been free to use it. Some people think that it should be illegal to use it compared with other drugs. To what extent do you agree or disagree?

** 첨삭은 **ieltseasywritng.com**